a cook's bible

GLUTEN-FREE, WHEAT-FREE
& DAIRY-FREE RECIPES

a cook's bible

GLUTEN-FREE, WHEAT-FREE & DAIRY-FREE RECIPES

MORE THAN 100 MOUTH-WATERING RECIPES FOR THE WHOLE FAMILY

GRACE CHEETHAM

DUNCAN BAIRD PUBLISHERS
LONDON

a cook's bible
Gluten-Free, Wheat-Free & Dairy-Free Recipes
Grace Cheetham

Distributed in the USA and Canada by
Sterling Publishing Co., Inc.
387 Park Avenue South, New York, NY 10016-8810

This edition first published in the UK and USA
in 2007 by Duncan Baird Publishers Ltd
Sixth Floor, Castle House
75–76 Wells Street, London W1T 3QH

This edition published in 2009

Editor: Alison Bolus
Managing Designer: Daniel Sturges
Commissioned photography: William Lingwood
Food stylists: Lucy McKelvie, Fergal Connolly
    and Martha Dunkerley
Prop stylist: Helen Trent

Library of Congress Cataloging-in-Publication Data

Cheetham, Grace.
  A cook's bible : gluten-free, wheat-free & dairy-free recipes
: more than 100 mouth-watering recipes for the whole family /
Grace Cheetham.
     p. cm.
  Includes bibliographical references and index.
  ISBN 978-1-84483-811-0 (alk. paper)
  1. Gluten-free diet--Recipes. 2. Wheat-free diet--Recipes. 3.
Milk-free diet--Recipes. I. Title.
  RM237.86.C44 2009
  641.5'63--dc22
                                        2008046519

10 9 8 7 6 5 4

Typeset in Helvetica
Color reproduction by Scanhouse, Malaysia
Printed in China by Imago

For Peter

For information about custom editions, special sales, premium
and corporate purchases, please contact Sterling Special Sales
Department at 800-805-5489 or specialsales@sterlingpub.com.

Publisher's note: While every care has been taken in compiling
the recipes for this book, Duncan Baird Publishers, or any other
persons who have been involved in working on this publication,
cannot accept responsibility for any errors or omissions,
inadvertent or not, that might be found in the recipes or text, or
for any problems that may arise as a result of preparing one of
these recipes. It is important that you consult your doctor before
following any of the recipes or information contained in this book
if you have any special dietary requirements or medical
conditions. Ill or elderly people, babies, young children, and
women who are pregnant or breastfeeding should avoid the
recipes containing raw meat or uncooked eggs.

Notes on the recipes
- Use organic ingredients
- Use fresh, unsweetened soymilk, soy margarine, and
  soy yogurt
Unless otherwise stated:
- Use large eggs and medium-size fruit and vegetables
- Use fresh herbs
- 1 tsp. = 5ml   1 tbsp. = 15ml   1 cup = 240ml

Notes on the symbols
The food symbols refer to the recipes only, not to any serving
suggestions. They are used even when only a small amount of
an item is present, such as sugar in fish sauce, salt in tamari soy
sauce, yeast in vinegar, and seeds in sesame and canola oils.
Peanuts have been classed as nuts and pine nuts as seeds.
Also, date syrup, honey, and molasses have been classed as
sugars because they have a similar effect on blood sugar levels
to sugar, but the sugar symbol hasn't been used for wine, as the
varieties vary so significantly. A few of the recipes contain gluten:
These are clearly marked with the gluten symbol. Check the
manufacturer's labeling carefully before using any food or drink,
since the ingredients used by different brands do vary, especially
regarding small quantities of ingredients such as salt, sugar, or
oil, although be aware that manufacturers are not required to
detail minuscule quantities of ingredients.

contents

KEY TO SYMBOLS

 contains gluten

 contains yeast

 contains eggs

 contains nuts

 contains seeds

 contains salt

 contains sugar

introduction

Embarking on a restricted diet can seem so hard. Often the foods you

have to cut out of your diet are the ones you crave and think you can't

live without. You think your meals will be difficult to prepare, and boring.

But this book will show you how deliciously easy to prepare—and truly

enjoyable—they can be. Packed full of mouth-watering recipes, all simple

to make, it'll show you how to create fantastic food for your daily life. Here

are meals to enjoy at home with your family and friends or to pack up and

take with you. Flick through these pages and you'll find a delicious selection

of breakfasts, lunches, snacks, dinners, side dishes, and desserts. From

cookies and brownies to crepes and cupcakes, from spaghetti and sushi to

pasta and pizza, they're all here—and all specifically designed to suit your diet.

In the beginning

When I was first diagnosed with an intolerance to gluten, wheat, and dairy, I was devastated. I remember my father took me to a cafe after I had seen the doctor, and we stared at the menu in complete confusion. I couldn't have any of the breads, cakes or cookies or any of my favorite drinks. In the end I ordered a glass of apple juice and sat there miserably. And for a long time my culinary experiences were like this—a mixture of despair and bewilderment. Gradually, I became used to going without, although my diet was bland, boring, and very restricted. But over the years I started to experiment with cooking, learning to make meals that were naturally gluten-, wheat-, and dairy-free, and I worked out ones that I could not only eat at home but also take with me for the day, if necessary. I also started to try out different products from whole-food stores, delicatessens, and supermarkets: dairy-free milks, margarines, and cheeses; different flours and grains; and new flavorings and sauces. Eating became less of the flavorless rice cakes and more of the delicious breads, pizzas, cookies, cakes, and desserts you'll find here.

I've put the best of these recipes into this book, in the hope you will find many that you love. There's a range of recipes using alternative ingredients instead of gluten, wheat, or dairy, as well as recipes that are naturally free of these ingredients. Here are breakfasts ranging from vitamin-packed smoothies to sustaining hot dishes; lunches to take with you or to enjoy at home; snacks for when you want to treat yourself; dinners, including simple suppers you can prepare in minutes, family meals you'll all love, and indulgent feasts, with side dishes; and desserts for when you're feeling decadent. Mix and match to suit yourself—eat Blueberry and Banana Muffins in the afternoon, for example, rather than breakfast; nibble on Apricot, Mango, and Coconut Bars for breakfast, instead of later in the day, or have a blow-out lunch with any of the dinner recipes, such as Duck with Cherry and Juniper Sauce or Gnocchi with Mushroom and Pancetta Sauce. It's up to you!

Spinach Tart (see page 76)

introduction

introduction

Smoked Salmon, Shrimp, and Vegetable Sushi (see page 65)

Following a gluten-free, wheat-free, and/or dairy-free diet

Getting your head around and following a restrictive diet is hard. It can seem so very tiring, monotonous, and isolating. At first, the idea of having to prepare every single meal your-self feels utterly daunting. You long to be able to pick up a carry-out pizza or a sandwich from a deli and to share your family's or friends' food. But the benefits of sticking to your diet are so great that they do make it all worthwhile. I've written this book in the hope I'll be able to make it easy for you. I've purposely made all the recipes simple to follow and use. Many of them can be cooked in under half an hour—and some can be pulled together in minutes. Don't be alarmed by the prospect of making sushi, pizza, or bread, because you'll find they're all remarkably do-able, and I've often included short-cut methods, including using a food processor to whizz together pastry dough, cakes, or desserts. All the ingredients are easy to obtain, and all the recipes have symbols for immediate reference showing whether they contain gluten, yeast, eggs, nuts, seeds, salt, or sugar, even if it's only a small amount. For people who can eat gluten but not wheat, I've included a few recipes with gluten, but these are marked with the gluten symbol. You won't need a vast array of kitchen equipment to make this food, or great culinary expertise. What's more, these are delicious recipes you can share with your family or friends—from normal, everyday lunches to slap-up dinners and extravagant meals for special occasions.

On the plus side

One of the great benefits of following a diet such as this is that you are likely to eat far more healthily. By taking gluten, wheat, and dairy out of your diet, you will be forced to abandon much of the junk food available and to eat fresher, purer, more nutritious produce, which can only be a good thing. When your body reacts to the foods to which it is allergic or intolerant, it can go into defense mode, and can cause a range of symptoms including

introduction

nausea, vomiting, headaches, migraines, rashes, eczema, asthma attacks, anaphylactic shock, bloating, bowel problems, chronic fatigue, and depression. Your body can then counteract by producing extra adrenaline to fight the reaction and, in doing so, compromises your immune system. So, apart from avoiding the problem foods, the best thing you can do for your body is to build up your reserves of vitamins, minerals, and other essential nutrients, and generally support your immune system as much as possible.

While you can buy a good variety of foods specially adapted for this kind of diet, they often contain additives and preservatives, which can be damaging, and often have very little nutritional value. In contrast, I've used a lot of fresh fruit and vegetables throughout this book, as well as essential fatty-acid-rich oils and fructose instead of high-GI (glycemic index) sugar. I've also used less salt and fructose than normal. The Confit of Duck, for example, uses only a quarter of the normal amount of salt, and the cakes and desserts, particularly the chocolate ones, do not have the sickly-sweet taste of often over-sugared, store-bought products. By cooking the meals on the following pages, you can not only make a positive effect on your health and well-being by following your diet properly, but also benefit greatly from the nutritional excellence of healthy home cooking.

Getting started

The first thing to do is to make sure you have a basic collection of pans and dishes, measuring cups and spoons, and possibly a food processor, a stick blender, and/or an electric mixer. Then it's time to stock your pantry. You might want to try a few ingredients at a time, or just go on a full-on shopping spree, which will mean you'll have all the basics at hand and some great snacks and bites to munch on whenever you feel hungry.

(*opposite*) Raspberry Tartlets (see page 91)

Instead of flours containing gluten, I've used a variety of flours throughout the recipes. Rice flour and gram (or chickpea) flour are great alternatives in muffins, cakes, cookies, breads, and pastry, and have a lovely subtle taste. Cornmeal flour (a finer-milled version of polenta) has a more granular texture and a slightly sweeter flavor, and potato flour and millet flour are useful as fillers or thickeners. Very occasionally, I've used a couple of flours that contain gluten: barley flour has excellent binding properties, but I've used it in only small amounts, because the taste can be overpowering, and the classic rye flour is great for flavor and texture. If you can't tolerate gluten, you can use the gluten-free alternatives given in most of the recipes, and substitute one of the other breads for the rye bread.

There is now a fantastic selection of dairy-free products available. I've used soymilk throughout the recipes and highly recommend the fresh, sugar-free versions, as they taste much better than the longlife kinds, and they still last for a considerable amount of time in the refrigerator. If you like, you can always use goat or sheep milk instead (if you can tolerate them), or rice, oat (if you can tolerate gluten), or any of the nut milks. I've also used soy yogurt and soy cheeses (again, you can substitute goat or sheep), tofu, and soy margarines, which you can substitute with any of the dairy-free olive-oil spreads.

I've used olive oil throughout because it's easy to obtain and is also a very stable oil that can be heated to a high heat without any problems. But you can easily use canola oil at high temperatures, or any of the other nutritious oils, such as safflower or soybean oil, if you're not heating them to high temperatures, or hemp seed or flaxseed oil for salads.

I've also used fruit sugar, or fructose, which is basically unrefined sugar from fruit. This excellent alternative to normal refined sugar has a GI-level five times lower than sucrose. I've also used date syrup as it also has a low GI score and contains valuable nutrients.

It's well worth stocking up on dried fruits, and nuts and seeds because they can make all the difference to a recipe, as well as being great snack foods. Almonds and coconuts, in particular, are gems: they are packed with nutrients and utterly delicious, but are also great to bake with and to use in various forms to add a rich, intense flavor.

Stock up, too, on extracts, spices, and other flavorings, such as tamari (a wheat-free soy sauce) and gluten-, yeast-, and dairy-free bouillon powder. Legumes and beans are also fantastically useful: they can add inexpensive, comforting substance to any recipe, and are a great source of protein and fiber, as well as being low GI. Try haricot beans, lima beans, Puy lentils, chickpeas—the list goes on and on. Finally, fill your cupboards with polenta, rices (basmati, risotto, and whole-grain, in particular), rice wrappers and noodles, gluten-free and wheat-free pastas and noodles, and different types of flakes, such as oat, barley, rice, buckwheat, amaranth, and quinoa, and you'll have the base for all types of meals.

Sign up for an organic delivery program and enjoy the benefits of fresh, locally grown fruit and vegetables, meat, fish, and other basics, without the hassle of shopping or carting heavy bags home. It is vital that you avoid the added chemicals in non-organic food, particularly meat and fish, and eating organic food also enables you to eat more in tune with the seasons, bringing you nearer to the natural state of food that enriches our bodies. Try to eat as many salads, steamed and raw vegetables, and fruit as possible, as these will support your immune system immensely, to make additives and preservatives (which can have unpleasant side effects) a thing of the past, and to drink plenty of clean, pure water.

Additional help

Consult a nutritionist or naturopath, who will help you to identify any other problem foods, as well as advise you on health-enhancing supplements. Spoil yourself by indulging in complementary therapies, such as massage, acupuncture, healing—whatever helps you to find calm and happiness. But, above all, stick with the diet: you're bound to notice the benefits of reduced symptoms, as well as greatly enhanced health and vitality. Go for it!

basics

Use this chapter for all the basic recipes you'll need. Whether it's a simple

stock or pastry recipe, for example, or a fresh Tomato and Bell Pepper

Sauce, a rich Hollandaise Sauce, or a fiery Thai Green Curry Paste, they're

all here. You'll also find various bread recipes, all of which are easy to

make and useful for every day: to eat for breakfast, with soups, salads, or

pâtés, or whenever hunger hits and you need a filling snack. You'll find that

many of the recipes work slightly differently from standard ones that use

gluten, wheat, and dairy, due to the nature of the ingredients used here. But

don't worry—they do work! And once you've baked your own Soda Bread,

whipped up a Salmon and Shrimp Fish Pie with Béchamel Sauce or a Tarte

Tatin with gluten-free pastry, there'll be no looking back!

tomato and bell pepper sauce

Makes about 5$^1/_4$ cups.

1 Heat the broiler to high. Cut 3 red, orange, or yellow bell peppers (or a mixture of colors) in half lengthwise and remove the seeds and pith. Place, cut-side down, on a broiler rack and broil under the hot broiler 4 to 5 minutes until the skins are black. Put into a plastic food bag and leave 2 to 3 minutes. Remove the bell peppers from the bag, peel off the skins, and chop coarsely.

2 Meanwhile, with a sharp knife, cut a cross in the skins of 3$^1/_4$ pounds vine-ripened tomatoes, place in a large, heatproof bowl, and cover with boiling water. Leave to stand 2 to 3 minutes, then remove from the water and peel off the skins. Cut each tomato into 8 pieces.

3 Heat 2 tablespoons olive oil in a heavy-bottom saucepan over low heat. Add 1 finely chopped large onion and cook 2 to 3 minutes until turning golden. Add 2 chopped garlic cloves and cook 30 seconds, then stir in 1 tablespoon tomato paste, the bell peppers, and tomatoes.

4 Turn the heat up to medium and cook 15 to 20 minutes, until the sauce thickens and reduces. Season lightly with sea salt and freshly ground black pepper.

béchamel sauce

Makes about 2$^2/_3$ cups.

1 Place $^3/_4$ cup sugar-free soymilk, 1 chopped onion, $^1/_2$ chopped leek, and 2 bay leaves in a saucepan. Bring to a boil, then turn the heat down, cover with a lid, and leave to simmer 3 to 4 minutes. Remove from the heat and leave to infuse 20 minutes.

2 Melt 4 tablespoons dairy-free margarine in a heavy-bottom saucepan over low heat. Stir in $^1/_3$ cup plus 1 tablespoon gram flour and 4 tablespoons rice flour. Remove the pan from the heat.

3 Gradually stir in scant 2 cups Vegetable Stock (see page 25), or stock made with gluten-, yeast-, and dairy-free bouillon powder, then the infused milk, stirring all the time.

4 Return the pan to the heat and bring to the boil, stirring continuously. The sauce thickens as it gets hotter, and will become lumpy if you stop stirring; if that happens, beat with a whisk until smooth again.

5 Once the sauce boils, turn the heat down and leave to simmer very gently 10 minutes. Stir frequently to prevent it sticking to the pan. Stir in another $^1/_2$ to 1 cup stock to make a smooth sauce that is thick, but still runny. Season lightly with sea salt and freshly ground black pepper.

white wine sauce

Makes about 2$\frac{1}{3}$ cups.

1   Melt 2 tablespoons dairy-free margarine in a heavy-bottom saucepan over low heat. Stir in 6 tablespoons gram flour and 3 tablespoons rice flour; remove the pan from the heat.

2   Gradually stir in $\frac{1}{2}$ cup organic dry white wine, 6 tablespoons sugar-free soymilk, and $\frac{3}{4}$ cup Vegetable Stock (see page 25), or stock made with gluten-, yeast-, and dairy-free bouillon powder, stirring the sauce all the time.

3   Return the pan to the heat and bring to the boil, stirring continuously. The sauce thickens as it gets hotter, and will become lumpy if you stop stirring; if that happens, beat with a whisk until smooth again.

4   Once the sauce boils, turn the heat down and leave to simmer very gently 10 minutes. Stir frequently to prevent it sticking to the pan. Stir in another $\frac{1}{2}$ to 1 cup stock to make a smooth sauce that is thick, but still runny. Season lightly with sea salt and freshly ground black pepper.

hollandaise sauce

Makes about 1$\frac{1}{4}$ cups.

1   Pour 2 tablespoons white wine vinegar and 2 tablespoons water into a small saucepan and add 1 teaspoon ground white pepper. Bring to a boil, then turn the heat down and leave to simmer 2 to 3 minutes until the liquid reduces by half. Tip into a shallow bowl and leave until cool.

2   Place 4 egg yolks in a heatproof bowl and beat. Gradually whisk in the cool vinegar mixture, a little at a time, until thoroughly mixed in.

3   Place the bowl over a saucepan of gently simmering water, so the bowl rests on the rim of the pan and does not touch the water. Keep whisking the mixture in the bowl 3 to 4 minutes until it is as thick as you can get it.

4   Cut 7 tablespoons dairy-free margarine into small pieces and add a little at a time, whisking constantly.

5   Pour in 1 tablespoon lemon juice and quickly whisk again to mix in, taking care not to overheat, as the sauce will curdle. Season lightly with sea salt and ground white pepper and serve immediately.

sauces & pastes

ras el hanout

Makes about 4 tablespoons.

1 Heat a heavy-bottom skillet over low heat. Add 1 teaspoon each cumin seeds and coriander seeds and dry-fry 2 to 3 minutes until they start to brown; keep the seeds moving all the time so they do not burn.

2 Remove the pan from the heat and grind the seeds to a fine powder using a mortar and pestle or stick blender attachment; place in a small bowl.

3 Add 2 teaspoons each sweet smoked paprika and ground ginger, 1 teaspoon each turmeric and ground cinnamon and ½ teaspoon each cayenne pepper, freshly grated nutmeg, ground cloves, ground allspice, sea salt, and freshly ground black pepper.

4 Stir well to mix together, then transfer to a clean storage jar with a tight-fitting lid. Keep in a cool, dark place 5 to 6 months and use as required.

thai green curry paste

Makes about 12 tablespoons.

1 Heat a heavy-bottom skillet over low heat. Add ½ tablespoon each cumin seeds and coriander seeds and dry-fry 2 to 3 minutes until they start to brown; keep the seeds moving all the time so they do not burn.

2 Remove the pan from the heat and grind the seeds to a fine powder using a mortar and pestle or stick blender attachment. Place in a blender or food processor.

3 Peel and coarsely chop the bottom half of 2 lemongrass stalks and add, along with 6 seeded and coarsely chopped large green chilies, 4 chopped shallots, a ¾-inch piece peeled and chopped fresh gingerroot, and 4 chopped garlic cloves; blend well.

4 Add 5 chopped kaffir lime leaves (or a strip of lime peel), 2 teaspoons shrimp paste, and 6 chopped cilantro stems with roots and leaves, or 1 small handful coarsely chopped cilantro leaves and stems, then blend until a coarse paste forms. Put in an airtight container and store in the refrigerator up to 1 week.

rich piecrust dough

1 Sift ¹/₂ cup rice flour, ³/₄ cup plus 1¹/₂ tablespoons gram flour, 4 tablespoons barley flour, and ¹/₂ teaspoon sea salt into a large mixing bowl. Cut ¹/₂ cup chilled dairy-free margarine into small cubes and, using cold fingertips, rub it into the flours until the mixture resembles fine bread crumbs.

2 Make a well in the middle and add 1 beaten extra-large egg, mixing lightly with a round-bladed knife so the dough begins to hold together. It needs to form a dough with a little extra moisture at the bottom of the bowl. If it is too dry, gradually add 1 to 2 tablespoons chilled water to make it quite sticky; if too sticky, add some rice flour.

3 Shape the dough into a ball; wrap in waxed paper and put in the refrigerator 30 minutes. This amount will line a 10-inch tart pan, 1¹/₄ inches deep, or five 5-inch tartlet pans, ³/₄ inch deep.

4 The dough can also be made in a food processor. Simply tip the sifted flours and salt into the bowl, add the margarine, and blend until the mixture resembles fine bread crumbs. Add the egg and blend for 20–30 seconds until the mixture comes together to form a sticky dough, adding a little extra water if needed.

rich piecrust dough (gluten-free)

1 Sift ¹/₂ cup rice flour, ³/₄ cup plus 1¹/₂ tablespoons gram flour, 3 tablespoons buckwheat flour, and ¹/₂ teaspoon sea salt into a large mixing bowl. Cut ¹/₂ cup chilled dairy-free margarine into small cubes and, using cold fingertips, rub it into the flours until the mixture resembles fine bread crumbs.

2 Make a well in the middle and add 1 beaten extra-large egg, mixing lightly with a round-bladed knife so the dough begins to hold together. It needs to form a dough with a little extra moisture at the base of the bowl. If it is too dry, gradually add 1 to 2 tablespoons chilled water to make it quite sticky; if too sticky, add some rice flour.

3 Shape the dough into a ball; wrap in waxed paper and put in the refrigerator for 30 minutes. This amount will line a 10-inch tart pan, 1¹/₄ inches deep, or five 5-inch tartlet pans, ³/₄ inch deep.

4 The pastry can also be made in a food processor (see left).

5 Note that this dough is very fragile and needs to be handled with great care. Roll it out quickly and smoothly, use a board to turn it into the pan, and use your fingertips to mold it together if it cracks a little when you turn it into the pan.

pastry

sweet rich piecrust dough

1   Sift ⅓ cup plus 1½ tablespoons rice flour and ¾ cup gram flour into a large mixing bowl. Stir in ½ cup finely ground blanched almonds and 3 tablespoons fruit sugar. Cut 5½ tablespoons chilled dairy-free margarine into small cubes and, using cold fingertips, rub it into the dry ingredients until the mixture resembles fine bread crumbs.

2   Make a well in the middle and add 1 beaten extra-large egg, mixing lightly with a round-bladed knife so the dough begins to hold together. It needs to form a dough with a little extra moisture at the bottom of the bowl. If it is too dry, gradually add 1–2 tablespoons chilled water to make it quite sticky; if too sticky, add some rice flour.

3   Shape the dough into a ball; wrap in waxed paper and put in the refrigerator 30 minutes. This amount will line a 10-inch tart pan, 1¼ inches deep, or five 5-inch tartlet pans, ¾ inch deep.

4   The dough can also be made in a food processor (see Rich Piecrust Dough), adding the ground almonds and sugar with the sifted flours.

tarte tatin pastry dough

1   Sift ⅓ cup plus 1½ tablespoons rice flour, ½ cup gram flour, and ½ cup finely ground blanched almonds into a large mixing bowl and stir in 5 tablespoons fruit sugar. Cut 5 tablespoons chilled dairy-free margarine into small pieces and, using cold fingertips, rub it into the dry ingredients until the mixture resembles fine bread crumbs.

2   Make a well in the middle and add 1 beaten extra-large egg, mixing lightly with a round-bladed knife so the dough begins to hold together. Continue adding the egg gradually until it is all mixed in and the mixture begins to come together to form a sticky dough.

3   Shape the dough into a ball; wrap in waxed paper and put in the refrigerator at least 30 minutes. This amount will line a 10-inch tart pan, 1¼ inches deep, or five 5-inch tartlet pans, ¾ inch deep.

4   The dough can also be made in a food processor (see Rich Piecrust Dough), adding the ground almonds and sugar with the sifted flours.

rye bread

1. Crumble 1 ounce fresh yeast, if using, into 1 cup warm water and leave to proof 10 minutes.
2. Sift 3 cups plus 1 tablespoon rye flour, $^1/_2$ cup rice flour, $^3/_4$ cup plus 1$^1/_2$ tablespoons gram flour, 4 tablespoons barley flour, $^2/_3$ cup pumpkin seeds, and $^1/_2$ teaspoon salt into a large mixing bowl. If not using fresh yeast, add a $^1/_4$-ounce envelope rapid-rise dry yeast.
3. Make a well in the middle and pour in 2 tablespoons date syrup and the proofed yeast, if using. Gradually draw the flour into the liquid using a wooden spoon, mixing well to form a soft dough. If it feels dry, add extra water, 1 tablespoon at a time; if sticky, add rye flour.
4. Turn out the dough onto a surface dusted with rye flour and knead 10 minutes until smooth and elastic. Return to the bowl, cover with a damp dish towel, and leave until it doubles in size—about 1 hour.
5. Lightly grease a baking sheet with dairy-free margarine. Turn out the dough and knead 2 minutes; shape into a loaf and place on the baking sheet. Cover and leave to rise 45 to 60 minutes. Preheat the oven to 400°F.
6. Bake 35 to 40 minutes until it is brown on top and sounds hollow when tapped on the bottom; transfer to a wire rack to cool.

soda bread

1. Preheat the oven to 400°F. Lightly grease a baking sheet with dairy-free margarine. Sift $^3/_4$ cup potato flour, $^1/_2$ cup plus 1 tablespoon gram flour, and $^3/_4$ cup plus 2$^1/_2$ tablespoons rice flour into a large mixing bowl and stir in $^1/_2$ teaspoon salt and 1 teaspoon baking soda. Cut 2 tablespoons chilled dairy-free margarine into small cubes and, using cold fingertips, rub it into the flours until the mixture resembles fine bread crumbs.
2. Make a well in the middle and pour in 1 beaten extra-large egg and $^1/_2$ cup sugar-free soymilk. Mix well with a wooden spoon until all the ingredients are well combined, then bring together with your hands to form a ball of dough.
3. Turn out the dough onto a surface dusted with rice flour and knead briefly, making sure there are not any lumps. Shape the dough into a flattened ball and place on the prepared baking sheet. Cut a cross about $^1/_2$ inch deep on the top.
4. Bake in the hot oven 30 to 35 minutes until it is light brown and risen and sounds hollow when tapped on the bottom; transfer to a wire rack and leave to cool completely before serving.

breads

cornbread

1 Preheat the oven to 400°F. Lightly grease a 9- x 5-inch bread pan with dairy-free margarine.

2 Sift 1 cup cornmeal and $^3/_4$ cup plus $2^1/_2$ tablespoons rice flour into a large mixing bowl and stir in 1 teaspoon gluten-free baking powder and 1 teaspoon salt. Cut 4 tablespoons chilled dairy-free margarine into small pieces and, using cold fingertips, rub it into the flour until the mixture resembles bread crumbs.

3 In a small bowl, beat 2 extra-large eggs and mix in $1^1/_3$ cups sugar-free soymilk. Make a well in the middle of the flour mixture and pour the liquid into it, stirring thoroughly with a wooden spoon to incorporate all the flour into the liquid to make a smooth batter.

4 Pour the batter into the prepared bread pan and bake in the hot oven 35 to 40 minutes until risen and golden brown. To check if it is baked through, insert a skewer into the middle of the loaf: if it comes out clean, the cornbread is baked; transfer to a wire rack and leave to cool completely before serving.

chicken stock

Makes $1^1/_2$ to $1^3/_4$ quarts.

1 Break up 1 large chicken carcass and place in a large saucepan. Add 1 chopped onion, the chopped white part of 1 leek, 1 chopped celery stalk, 1 chopped large carrot, 6 parsley stems, 1 bay leaf, 1 thyme sprig, 6 peppercorns, $^1/_2$ teaspoon sea salt, and 2 quarts water.

2 Bring to a boil, then turn the heat down, cover with a lid, and leave to simmer 3 hours. Leave the stock to cool, then strain into a non-metallic container.

3 As soon as the stock is completely cool, remove and discard the layer of fat that will have separated out and be sitting on the surface. Unless you are using the stock immediately, cover and store in the refrigerator 2 to 3 days, or freeze for later use.

fish stock

Makes about 3 quarts.

1 Wash $4^1/_2$ pounds fish bones (preferably from white fish) thoroughly and break up. Place in a large saucepan with 1 chopped onion, the chopped white part of 1 leek, 1 chopped large carrot, 6 parsley stems, 6 peppercorns, $^1/_2$ teaspoon sea salt, and 3 quarts water.

2 Bring to a boil, then turn the heat down, cover with a lid, and leave to simmer 40 minutes. Leave to cool, then strain into a non-metallic container.

3 When the stock is cold, cover and store in the refrigerator 1 to 2 days, or freeze for later use.

vegetable stock

Makes 1 to $1^1/_4$ quarts.

1 Place 2 chopped onions, the chopped white part of 2 leeks, 2 chopped celery stalks, 3 chopped large carrots, 1 small handful parsley stems, 2 bay leaves, 12 peppercorns, $^1/_2$ teaspoon sea salt, and $1^1/_2$ quarts water in a large saucepan.

2 Bring to a boil, then turn the heat down, cover with a lid, and leave to simmer 40 minutes. Leave to cool, then strain into a non-metallic container.

3 When the stock is cold, cover and store in the refrigerator 3 to 4 days, or freeze for later use.

stocks

breakfasts

Flick through these pages and you'll find a mouth-watering selection of

breakfasts to savor, from quick bites on the run to more leisurely meals.

Here are juices and smoothies, mueslis, crepes and muffins, omelets, and

full breakfasts. Dive into a Summer Berry Smoothie, which can be made in

minutes, or a Blueberry and Banana Muffin, which you can take with you

as you head out, for example, or kick back and enjoy Scrambled Eggs with

Bacon, and freshly baked bread. Start your day with a nutrient-rich meal and

you'll feel the difference immediately—your energy levels will soar, you'll

feel more alert and focused, and you won't be so tempted to eat forbidden

snacks throughout the day.

summer berry smoothie

PREPARATION TIME **5 MINUTES, PLUS 30 MINUTES THAWING TIME**   SERVES **2**

heaped 4 cups raspberries, strawberries, blueberries, and/or red currants, or 1 large bag frozen mixed summer berries

¹⁄₃ cup silken tofu, cut into small chunks
2 cups soymilk
1 to 2 tablespoons honey

1   If using frozen berries, take out of the freezer and leave to stand at room temperature about 30 minutes, to thaw slightly, before making the smoothie.
2   Put all the berries and/or currants into a blender or food processor. Add the tofu, milk, and honey to taste and blend until smooth and creamy. Pour into glasses and serve.

breakfasts

mango, passionfruit, and banana smoothie

PREPARATION TIME **5 MINUTES**   SERVES **2**

1 large ripe mango
2 passionfruits, cut in half
1 banana, thickly sliced

1   With a sharp knife, carefully slice the mango down the sides, avoiding the stone. Cut the flesh inside the slices into small squares, cutting down to the peel but not piercing it, and scoop out with a spoon. Peel the remains of the mango and slice the flesh from the seed. Place all the mango flesh in a blender or food processor.
2   Scoop out the pulp and seeds from the passionfruits and add to the mango with the banana.
3   Blend until smooth and creamy, then pour into glasses and serve.

pineapple, nectarine, and ginger juice

PREPARATION TIME **5 MINUTES**   SERVES **2**

1 large ripe pineapple
4 ripe nectarines or peaches, pitted and cut into quarters
1¼-inch piece fresh gingerroot, peeled and coarsely chopped

1   Trim the woody base and green top off the pineapple and, holding it upright, slice off and discard the skin, including the "eyes." Slice the flesh down the length of the fruit all around into long, thin slices, stopping when you reach the core.

2   Press the pineapple and nectarine pieces with the chopped ginger through an electric juicer. Pour into glasses and serve.

pomegranate, grape, and kiwi juice

PREPARATION TIME **10 MINUTES**   SERVES **2**

2 pomegranates, cut in half
1 large bunch seedless grapes, about 1½ pounds total weight, destalked
2 kiwi fruits, cut in half

1   Hold each pomegranate half above a large mixing bowl and bash the outer skin with the back of a wooden spoon, so the fleshy red seeds fall into the bowl. You'll need to bash the skin a few times before the seeds begin to fall out, but they will.

2   Set aside 2 tablespoons of the seeds, then press the remainder with the grapes and kiwi fruits through an electric juicer. Pour into glasses, add the reserved seeds, and serve.

muesli with almond milk

PREPARATION TIME **10 MINUTES, PLUS OVERNIGHT SOAKING TIME**   SERVES **4**

1²/₃ cups jumbo rolled oats

heaped ¹/₃ cup barley flakes

¹/₂ cup coarsely chopped hazelnuts

¹/₃ cup coarsely chopped almonds

¹/₃ cup coarsely chopped sugar-free dried mango

¹/₃ cup sugar-free dried cranberries

¹/₃ cup coarsely chopped sugar-free dried figs

3 tablespoons flax seed

Almond milk:

scant 1²/₃ cups whole blanched almonds

1 to 2 tablespoons honey

1   To make the almond milk, place the blanched almonds in a bowl, cover with scant 3¹/₄ cups water, and leave to soak overnight or at least 12 hours.

2   The next day, put the almonds in a blender, add ¹/₂ cup of the soaking liquid, and blend. With the motor running, pour the remaining liquid in gradually and the honey to taste, blending thoroughly to a fine milk. (This will make about 1 quart.) You can store the almond milk in an airtight container in the refrigerator up to 3 days.

3   In a large mixing bowl, combine all the dry ingredients, then spoon into bowls. Serve with the almond milk, or use soymilk, if you prefer.

To make a gluten-free version of this muesli, you can use heaped ²/₃ cup rice flakes and ²/₃ cup buckwheat flakes instead of the oats and barley flakes. Alternatively, you could try 2 cups quinoa flakes.

VARIATION

bircher muesli

PREPARATION TIME **5 MINUTES, PLUS OVERNIGHT SOAKING TIME**   SERVES **4**

muesli

2 cups oatmeal

1¹/₂ cups apple juice

2 apples

¹/₃ cup chopped sugar-free dried apple

¹/₂ cup soy yogurt

heaped ¹/₃ cup seasonal berries, such as raspberries and blueberries

1 Put the oats in a large mixing bowl and pour the apple juice over to cover. Cover the bowl and leave to soak overnight in the refrigerator.

2 In the morning, peel and grate the apples and add them to the oatmeal mixture. Stir in the dried apple and yogurt.

3 Spoon the mixture into bowls. Scatter the berries over each helping and serve.

To make a gluten-free version of bircher muesli, you can use 1²/₃ cups buckwheat flakes instead of the oats. Alternatively, you could try 2¹/₄ cups quinoa flakes, but you will need an extra scant ²/₃ cup apple juice.

VARIATION

crepes with toasted coconut flakes and date syrup

PREPARATION TIME **5 MINUTES, PLUS 30 MINUTES STANDING TIME**
COOKING TIME **15 TO 20 MINUTES**   SERVES **4**

breakfasts

1/4 cup plus 1 tablespoon rice flour

1/2 cup gram flour

1 pinch salt

1 egg, beaten

1 cup soymilk

1 1/2 cups unsweetened coconut flakes

1 tablespoon dairy-free margarine

3 tablespoons date syrup

1 Sift the flours with the salt into a large mixing bowl. Make a well in the middle and add the egg, beating slowly with a wooden spoon to incorporate the flours. Slowly beat in the milk, gradually drawing in the flours to form a smooth batter. Cover and leave to stand at least 10 minutes, or up to 30 minutes in the refrigerator.

2 Meanwhile, heat an 8-inch heavy-bottom skillet over medium heat until hot. Toss in the coconut flakes and dry-fry until light brown, turning frequently to prevent burning; tip the coconut into a bowl. Wipe the skillet clean and return it to the heat. Add the margarine and melt, making sure it covers the bottom of the pan.

3 Pour 1/2 cup prepared batter into the pan and tilt the pan so the bottom is completely covered with the batter. (It needs to be thicker than for a normal crepe because of the lack of gluten to hold it together.) Cook 2 to 3 minutes until the bottom of the crepe is golden. Using a wooden spatula, carefully loosen the crepe from the bottom, then flip it over onto the other side (or toss it if you are feeling confident). Cook 1 to 2 minutes longer.

4 Repeat with the remaining batter, stacking the freshly cooked crepes between sheets of nonstick baking parchment paper to prevent them sticking together and keep them warm. Note that the later crepes will take only 1 to 2 minutes on each side, because the pan will be hot.

5 When all 4 crepes are cooked, fold them into quarters, drizzle a little date syrup over the top, sprinkle with the toasted coconut flakes, and serve.

blueberry and banana muffins

PREPARATION TIME **10 MINUTES**   COOKING TIME **20 TO 25 MINUTES**   MAKES **10**

5 tablespoons dairy-free margarine, softened,
   plus extra for greasing
¹/₄ cup fruit sugar
1 extra-large egg, lightly beaten
scant ¹/₂ cup soymilk

¹/₂ cup plus 1¹/₂ tablespoons rice flour
³/₄ cup plus 4 tablespoons gram flour
1 teaspoon gluten-free baking powder
2 small bananas, mashed
1 cup blueberries

1   Heat the oven to 400°F. Grease 10 paper muffin liners and place them in a muffin tray.
    Put the margarine and sugar in a large mixing bowl and, using an electric mixer, beat well
    until light and fluffy. Gradually beat in the egg, a little at a time, then beat in the soymilk.

2   Sift in the flours and baking powder and stir quickly with a wooden spoon until mixed;
    do not overmix, and don't worry if you can still see lumps in the mixture.

3   Carefully fold in the mashed bananas and the blueberries, then spoon the mixture into the
    prepared paper cases, filling each one about two-thirds full.

4   Bake in the hot oven 20 to 25 minutes until well risen and just firm to the touch, or until a
    skewer inserted into the middle comes out clean. Take the muffins out of the oven and
    either eat them warm or transfer them to a wire rack to cool in their paper liners.

herb omelet with creamy mushrooms

PREPARATION TIME **5 MINUTES**   COOKING TIME **10 MINUTES**   SERVES **2**

4 eggs

1 tablespoon plus 1 teaspoon dairy-free margarine

2 heaped tablespoons chopped mint leaves

2 heaped tablespoons chopped basil leaves

2 tablespoons olive oil

heaped 1³/₄ cups button mushrooms, cut into quarters

³/₄ cup plus 2 tablespoons soy yogurt

sea salt and freshly ground black pepper

1   Beat the eggs in a bowl, then season lightly with salt and pepper. Heat the margarine in an 8-inch heavy-bottom skillet, making sure the bottom is well covered in the hot fat. Pour the egg mixture into the pan and sprinkle half the chopped mint and basil over. As the egg begins to set, keep lifting the edges gently and tilting the pan to let the uncooked egg trickle underneath. After 5 to 6 minutes the bottom of the omelet will be golden and the top almost set, but still soft.

2   Meanwhile, heat the oil in a large, heavy-bottom saucepan. Add the mushrooms and cook over medium heat 3 to 4 minutes, stirring frequently. Using a whisk or electric mixer, blend the yogurt. Turn the heat down to low, pour the yogurt into the pan, add the remaining herbs, and season lightly with salt and pepper. Gently cook the mixture 2 to 3 minutes, making sure not to cook it for too long, because the yogurt can curdle.

3   When the omelet is just set, tilt the pan away from you and, using a metal spatula, carefully fold it in half. Leave it to stand 30 seconds, then cut into 2 portions. Serve immediately with the creamy mushrooms.

scrambled eggs with bacon

PREPARATION TIME **5 MINUTES**   COOKING TIME **6 MINUTES**   SERVES **4**

8 slices nitrate-free bacon

8 eggs

6 tablespoons sugar-free soymilk

4 tablespoons dairy-free margarine

sea salt and freshly ground black pepper

1   Preheat the broiler to high. Place the bacon on the broiler rack and cook under the hot
     broiler 2 to 3 minutes on each side, or until cooked to your liking.

2   While the bacon is cooking, beat the eggs in a small mixing bowl. Stir in the soymilk
     and season lightly with salt and pepper. Melt the margarine in a heavy-bottom saucepan
     over very low heat. Pour in the egg mixture and cook very gently, stirring frequently,
     4 to 5 minutes until the mixture thickens, but is still slightly runny.

3   Serve immediately with the bacon and with slices of toast of your choice (see bread recipes
     on pages 23–4).

baked beans with hash browns

PREPARATION TIME **20 MINUTES, PLUS OVERNIGHT SOAKING TIME**   COOKING TIME **1½ TO 2 HOURS**   SERVES **2**

scant ²/₃ cup dried haricot beans, or 1 can (14-ounce)
    salt-free haricot beans in water,
    drained and rinsed
4 vine-ripened tomatoes
1 tablespoon olive oil
1 onion, chopped
6 tablespoons tomato paste
1 tablespoon chopped thyme leaves
sea salt

Hash browns:
4 potatoes, peeled and grated
1 small onion, grated
1 egg, beaten
1 tablespoon rice flour
1 teaspoon sea salt
1 tablespoon olive oil

1   If using dried haricot beans, place in a bowl, cover with cold water, and leave to soak over-night or at least 12 hours.

2   The next day, drain the beans and rinse thoroughly. Put in a large saucepan, cover with fresh water, and bring to a boil. Boil rapidly 10 minutes, then turn the heat down, cover with a lid, and leave to simmer 1 to 1½ hours until tender; drain thoroughly.

3   Meanwhile, cut a cross in the skin of each tomato with a sharp knife, place in a heatproof bowl, and cover with boiling water. Leave to stand 2 minutes, then remove the tomatoes, peel off and discard the skins, and coarsely chop the flesh.

4   Heat the oil in a heavy-bottom saucepan over medium heat. Add the onion and cook 2 to 3 minutes until golden. Add the remaining ingredients, including the beans, and ¹/₂ cup water, bring to a boil, stir well, then turn the heat down, cover with a lid, and leave to simmer 30 minutes; adjust the seasoning, if necessary.

5   Meanwhile, make the hash browns. Mix the potatoes and onion in a bowl. Tip the mixture onto a clean dish towel, wrap it around the mixture and squeeze well so it soaks up the excess moisture. Return to the bowl, stir in the egg, flour, and salt, and mix well.

6   Divide the mixture into 6 portions and shape each into a small, round cake. Heat the oil in a heavy-bottom skillet over medium heat. Place 3 of the hash browns in the pan, flatten them slightly with the back of a wooden spoon, and cook 5 to 6 minutes on each side until crisp and golden brown. Remove from the pan with a spatula and keep warm; repeat with the remaining hash browns. Serve with the baked beans.

hot dishes

lunches

Wherever you are and whatever you're doing, you'll find exactly the recipe

you need in the following pages. Whether you want to pack something into

a lunchbox or take a bite for a picnic, you'll discover pâtés, potato cakes,

and tabbouleh. If you feel like having soup—either a hearty, warming one

such as Pea and Ham Soup or a light Chilled Avocado Soup for a summer's

day—you'll find a delicious selection here. There are salads, from Thai-Style

Chicken Salad with Rice Vermicelli to Oven-Roasted Butternut Squash and

Beet Salad, and delicious, comforting favorites, such as Prosciutto and

Arugula Pizza, as well as more exotic dishes, such as Shrimp and Vegetable

Tempura. Many of these recipes can be prepared in advance and stored,

or they can be made quickly in the morning before you leave for the day.

smoked salmon pâté

PREPARATION TIME **3 TO 5 MINUTES**   SERVES **2**

9 ounces smoked salmon

heaped ¹/₂ cup chopped silken tofu

1 tablespoon sugar-free soymilk

juice of ¹/₂ lemon

1 handful dill, finely chopped, plus extra to serve

freshly ground black pepper

1   Place all the ingredients in a bowl and blend briefly using a stick blender to form a coarse paste. Alternatively, blend all the ingredients in a blender or food processor.

2   Serve spread thickly on slices of bread (see pages 23–4) and topped with dill, or put in a container for a lunchbox.

VARIATION

For an Asian-style pâté, replace the milk, lemon, dill, and pepper with ¹/₂ to 1 large fresh seeded and finely chopped red chili, ¹/₂-inch piece peeled and finely chopped fresh gingerroot, 1 large chopped garlic clove, and the juice of 1 lime.

potato cakes with smoked salmon

PREPARATION TIME **10 MINUTES**   COOKING TIME **30 TO 40 MINUTES**   SERVES **2**

9 ounces potatoes, peeled and cut into chunks

4 tablespoons dairy-free margarine

3 tablespoons rice flour, plus extra for dusting

5 tablespoons gram flour

$^1/_2$ teaspoon sea salt

1 teaspoon gluten-free baking powder

1 extra-large egg, beaten

2 tablespoons olive oil

9 ounces smoked salmon

1   Put the potatoes in a saucepan and cover with cold water. Place over high heat and bring to a boil, then turn the heat down, cover with a lid and leave to simmer 15 to 20 minutes until tender. Drain and mash the potatoes well with the margarine until smooth.

2   Sift the flours into a large mixing bowl. Stir in the salt and baking powder and make a well in the middle of the mixture. Pour the beaten egg into the well, then add the mashed potato and, using a wooden spoon, gradually draw the flour mixture into the egg and potato, mixing until all the ingredients are thoroughly combined.

3   Turn the mixture out onto a surface that has been liberally dusted with rice flour; divide into six portions. With cold hands, shape each portion into a ball, then flatten to form a round cake and dust lightly with more rice flour. You'll find the mixture sticky, so try to work quickly before your hands warm up and keep sprinkling more rice flour onto the work surface whenever you need to.

4   Heat half of the oil in a large, heavy-bottom skillet. Add 3 of the potato cakes and cook 4 to 5 minutes on each side until golden brown. Remove the potato cakes from the pan, drain on paper towels, then transfer to a wire rack to cool while you cook the second batch.

5   Top each potato cake with a slice of smoked salmon and serve. Alternatively, leave to cool completely and put in a container for a lunchbox.

artichoke pâté

PREPARATION TIME **15 MINUTES**   COOKING TIME **1 TO 40 MINUTES**   SERVES **4**

8 artichokes, stems and very outer leaves removed,
**   or 14 ounces bottled or canned artichoke hearts**
**   in water or oil, drained (1 tablespoon oil reserved)**
1 tablespoon olive oil (optional)

2 garlic cloves, chopped
1 ounce coarsely chopped arugula (optional)
sea salt

1 If using fresh artichokes, place in 2 large saucepans of boiling water and return to a boil, then turn the heat down, cover with a lid, and leave to simmer 30 to 40 minutes until you can pull the leaves off the artichokes easily. Drain, leave until cool enough to handle, and remove all the leaves, then scrape out the hairy "chokes," leaving the bottoms, known as the "hearts."

2 If using artichokes preserved in oil, use 1 tablespoon oil from the bottle or can; if not, use olive oil. Heat the oil in a small, heavy-bottom saucepan. Add the garlic and cook 30 seconds until just starting to brown. Tip into a bowl, add the artichoke hearts and arugula, if using, and blend with a stick blender to form a smooth, creamy paste; season lightly with salt. Alternatively, blend in a blender or food processor.

3 Spread on slices of bread (see pages 23–4), or put in a container for a lunchbox.

quinoa tabbouleh

PREPARATION TIME **10 MINUTES**   COOKING TIME **15 TO 20 MINUTES**   SERVES **4**

³/₄ cup quinoa

4 vine-ripened tomatoes

2 bunches flat-leaf parsley, finely chopped

2 bunches mint, finely chopped

6 scallions, finely sliced

Dressing:

6 tablespoons extra virgin olive oil

juice of 2 lemons

sea salt and freshly ground black pepper

1   Place the quinoa in a strainer and rinse well under cold running water, then transfer to a saucepan and pour 1 cup cold water over. Bring to a boil, then turn the heat down, cover with a lid, and leave to simmer 15 to 20 minutes until the quinoa is tender and the water is absorbed; transfer to a serving bowl and leave to cool. (If any water is left in the pan, drain the quinoa thoroughly through a strainer first.)

2   Meanwhile, with a sharp knife, make a cross in the skin of each tomato, then place in a large, heatproof bowl, and cover with boiling water; leave to stand 2 to 3 minutes. Drain, then peel off and discard the skins. Halve each tomato, scoop out and discard the seeds, then dice the flesh and add to the quinoa in the bowl. Stir in the parsley, mint, and scallions.

3   Whisk together the dressing ingredients in a measuring cup or a bowl and season lightly, then pour over the top of the tabbouleh, stirring thoroughly so the ingredients are well combined. Serve or put in a container for a lunchbox.

pea and ham soup

PREPARATION TIME **10 MINUTES**   COOKING TIME **20 MINUTES**
ADDITIONAL TIME **MAKING THE STOCK**   SERVES **4**

2 tablespoons olive oil

1 onion, finely chopped

2 large garlic cloves, chopped

1 carrot, peeled and chopped

$^1/_2$ large or 1 small leek, chopped

5 cups fresh or frozen shelled peas

1 bay leaf

$1^1/_4$ quarts Chicken or Vegetable Stock (see pages 24–5), or vegetable stock made from gluten-, yeast-, and dairy-free bouillon powder

9 ounces nitrate-free air-dried ham, such as Serrano, chopped

sea salt and freshly ground black pepper

1   Heat the oil in a large, heavy-bottom saucepan over low heat. Add the onion and cook 2 to 3 minutes until just starting to turn golden brown. Stir in the garlic, then add the carrot and leek and cook one minute, stirring occasionally.

2   Add the peas and the bay leaf and cook 5 minutes, then pour in the stock. Turn up the heat slightly and bring to a low boil, then turn the heat down, cover with a lid, and leave to simmer 5 minutes. Stir in half the ham, using all the pieces with any fat on them, and cook 5 minutes.

3   Remove the bay leaf, then blend the mixture briefly in the pan using a stick blender to make a coarsely textured soup. Alternatively, blend the soup in a blender or food processor, return to the pan, and heat through. Stir in the remaining ham, season lightly with salt and pepper, and serve with slices of bread (see pages 23–4).

tom yum soup

PREPARATION TIME **10 MINUTES**   COOKING TIME **25 MINUTES**
ADDITIONAL TIME **MAKING THE STOCK**   SERVES **4**

1/2-inch piece fresh gingerroot, peeled and chopped

1 heaped tablespoon chopped cilantro leaves and
   stems, plus whole leaves to serve

1 shallot, chopped

2 large fresh red chilies, seeded and chopped

1 tablespoon olive oil

6 lemongrass stalks, white ends sliced

2 tablespoons Thai fish sauce

2 quarts Vegetable Stock (see page 25), or stock
   made from gluten-, yeast-, and dairy-free
   bouillon powder

heaped 1 cup sliced button mushrooms

9 ounces cooked, shelled shrimp

juice of 1 lime

1 Put the ginger, cilantro, shallot, chilies, and oil in a food processor and blend to form a
   coarse paste. Tip the mixture into a large, heavy-bottom saucepan and add the lemongrass, fish sauce, and stock. Bring to a boil over medium heat, then turn the heat down,
   cover with a lid, and leave to simmer 15 minutes.

2 Strain through a fine strainer and return to the cleaned pan. Add the mushrooms and return
   to a boil, then turn the heat down, cover with a lid, and leave to simmer 5 minutes. Add the
   shrimp and cook 1 to 2 minutes, then stir in the lime juice. Check the seasoning, adding
   more fish sauce, if required. Sprinkle with cilantro leaves and serve with slices of bread
   (see pages 23–4).

crab bisque

PREPARATION TIME **10 MINUTES**   COOKING TIME **35 MINUTES**
ADDITIONAL TIME **MAKING THE STOCK**   SERVES **4**

4 tablespoons dairy-free margarine

$^1/_2$ onion, chopped

1 celery stalk, chopped

1 carrot, peeled and chopped

1 bay leaf

1$^1/_4$ quarts Fish Stock (see page 25), or vegetable
    stock made from gluten-, yeast-, and dairy-free
    bouillon powder

scant $^1/_2$ cup organic dry white wine

2 vine-ripened tomatoes, coarsely chopped

1 tablespoon tomato paste

$^1/_4$ teaspoon cayenne pepper

1 pound cooked crabmeat, about half brown and
    half white meat

$^2/_3$ cup soy yogurt

sea salt and freshly ground black pepper

1   Melt the margarine in a large, heavy-bottom saucepan. Add the onion, celery, carrot, and
    bay leaf and cook over low heat 2 to 3 minutes. Stir in the stock, wine, chopped tomatoes,
    and tomato paste, increase the heat, and bring to a boil. Turn the heat down, cover with a
    lid, and leave to simmer 20 minutes; remove the bay leaf.

2   Blend the bisque in the pan using a stick blender. Alternatively, blend in a blender or food
    processor, return to the pan, and heat through. Stir in the cayenne and crabmeat and bring
    to a boil, then turn the heat down, cover with a lid, and leave to simmer 10 minutes; season
    lightly with salt and pepper.

3   Using a whisk or a stick blender, blend the yogurt until smooth, then add to the soup and
    stir in thoroughly. Serve with slices of bread (see pages 23–4).

zucchini and spicy seeds soup

PREPARATION TIME **10 MINUTES**   COOKING TIME **25 TO 35 MINUTES**
ADDITIONAL TIME **MAKING THE STOCK**   SERVES **4**

1½ tablespoons olive oil

1 onion, chopped

2 garlic cloves, chopped

4 large zucchini, about 1½ pounds total weight,
  thickly sliced

9 ounces potatoes, peeled and thickly sliced

2 cups Vegetable Stock (see page 25), or stock made
  from gluten-, yeast-, and dairy-free bouillon powder

½ to 1 teaspoon chili flakes

sea salt and freshly ground black pepper

Spicy seeds:

heaped ¾ cup sunflower seeds

⅔ cup sesame seeds

scant ½ cup pumpkin seeds

4 tablespoons tamari soy sauce

1   Preheat the oven to 300°F. Heat the oil in a large, heavy-bottom saucepan over low heat. Add the onion and cook 2 to 3 minutes until golden. Stir in the garlic, then add the zucchini and potatoes and cook 3 to 4 minutes, stirring occasionally. Pour in the stock and bring to a boil, then turn the heat down, cover with a lid, and leave to simmer 20 to 25 minutes until the potatoes are soft.

2   Meanwhile, prepare the spicy seeds. Spread the seeds over a baking tray and sprinkle with the tamari soy sauce; roast in the hot oven 15 minutes. Take the seeds out of the oven, turn them over, and return to the oven 10 to 15 minutes longer until golden brown.

3   Stir the spicy seeds into the soup with the chili flakes to taste. Blend briefly in the pan using a stick blender to make a coarsely textured soup or for longer for a smoother result. Alternatively, blend in a blender or food processor, then return to the pan and heat through. Season lightly with salt and pepper and serve with slices of bread (see pages 23–4).

VARIATION   For a lighter version of this soup, omit the potatoes and use only 1 cup stock and ¼ to ½ teaspoon chili flakes.

chilled avocado soup

PREPARATION TIME **10 MINUTES, PLUS 2 HOURS CHILLING TIME**
ADDITIONAL TIME **MAKING THE STOCK**   SERVES **4**

soups

5 ripe avocados, peeled, pitted, and chopped

1 shallot, finely chopped

1 large garlic clove, finely chopped

juice of 1 lemon

1 tablespoon olive oil

²/₃ cup soy yogurt

1²/₃ cups cold Chicken or Vegetable Stock (see

pages 24–5), or cold vegetable stock made from

gluten-, yeast-, and dairy-free bouillon powder

2 heaped tablespoons chopped mint leaves

sea salt and freshly ground black papper

1 Put the avocados, shallot, garlic, lemon juice, oil, and yogurt in a food processor and blend until smooth. With the motor running, gradually pour in the stock. Add half of the chopped mint and blend briefly to mix in; season lightly with salt and pepper.

2 Pour the soup into a large bowl, cover with plastic wrap, and leave in the refrigerator 2 hours.

3 Stir in the remaining mint and serve with slices of bread (see pages 23–4).

roast tomato and sage soup

PREPARATION TIME **10 MINUTES**   COOKING TIME **1½ HOURS**
ADDITIONAL TIME **MAKING THE STOCK**   SERVES **4**

16 large vine-ripened tomatoes,
    about 4 pounds total weight, cut in half

4 large garlic cloves, unpeeled

3 tablespoons olive oil

1 red onion, chopped

1½ tablespoons chopped sage leaves

½ cup Vegetable Stock (see page 25), or stock
    made from gluten-, yeast-, and dairy-free
    bouillon powder

sea salt and freshly ground black pepper

1   Preheat the oven to 350°F. Arrange the tomato halves, cut-side up, on a baking tray with the garlic cloves. Roast in the hot oven 1¼ hours until brown and soft; remove from the oven and leave to cool slightly.

2   Heat the oil in a large, heavy-bottom saucepan over low heat. Add the onion and cook 2 to 3 minutes until it starts to turn golden.

3   With a metal spoon, scrape the flesh away from the tomato skins and add to the saucepan, discarding the skins. Squeeze the flesh out of the garlic cloves and add to the pan, discarding the skins. Stir the chopped sage into the mixture and bring to a boil, then turn the heat down, cover with a lid, and leave to simmer 10 minutes, stirring occasionally.

4   Blend in the pan using a stick blender until smooth, adding the vegetable stock gradually until the soup is thick, but still runny. Alternatively, blend in a blender or food processor, then return to the pan and heat through. Season lightly with salt and pepper, and serve hot or chilled with slices of bread (see pages 23–4).

thai-style chicken salad with rice vermicelli

PREPARATION TIME **10 MINUTES**   COOKING TIME **30 TO 35 MINUTES**   SERVES **4**

2 skinless, boneless chicken breast halves

2 tablespoons olive oil

5 ounces rice vermicelli

4 scallions, finely sliced

1 garlic clove, finely chopped

³/₄-inch piece fresh gingerroot, peeled and
 finely chopped

¹/₂ large fresh red chili, seeded and finely chopped

1 handful chopped mint leaves

2 handfuls chopped cilantro leaves

1 handful chopped basil leaves

¹/₂ cucumber, cut into matchsticks

2 carrots, peeled and cut into matchsticks

1 zucchini, cut into matchsticks

juice of 1 lime

1 teaspoon Thai fish sauce

2 handfuls unsalted peanuts, chopped, to serve

1 Preheat the oven to 350°F. Put the chicken pieces in a baking dish, drizzle 1 tablespoon of the oil over, and cover. Cook in the hot oven 20 to 25 minutes until cooked through; to test that the chicken is cooked through, prick with the tip of a sharp knife and check that the juices run clear, not pink. Take the chicken out of the oven and leave to cool.

2 Put the vermicelli in a large heatproof bowl, cover with boiling water, and leave to stand 5 minutes until soft. Tip the noodles into a colander and rinse well under cold running water.

3 Heat a large wok or skillet over high heat until hot. Add the remaining oil and swirl it around the wok. Toss in the scallions and stir-fry about 1 minute until they start to turn golden. Add the garlic, ginger, and chili and cook 1 minute, then tip into a large salad bowl. Add the chopped herbs and the vegetable matchsticks.

4 Shred the cooled chicken and add to the bowl, along with the lime juice and fish sauce. Add the noodles and stir thoroughly until all the ingredients are well combined. Sprinkle with the peanuts and serve.

beef carpaccio

PREPARATION TIME **5 MINUTES**   SERVES **4**

1 pound beef tenderloin, very thinly sliced into
     about 12 slices
2 ounces baby leaf spinach
2 ounces arugula
1 large handful flat-leaf parsley, coarsely chopped
12 cherry tomatoes, cut in half horizontally

Dressing:
1 garlic clove, chopped
juice of $\frac{1}{2}$ lemon
4 tablespoons extra virgin olive oil
sea salt and freshly ground black pepper

1   Arrange the steak slices on a large piece of plastic wrap, making sure they are all separated, and cover with another piece of plastic wrap. Using a rolling pin, roll the slices of meat out until they become paper-thin.

2   Whisk together the dressing ingredients in a measuring cup or a bowl, seasoning lightly.

3   Serve the steak slices with the spinach, arugula, and parsley, and the tomato halves, all drizzled with the dressing.

borlotti bean and tuna salad

PREPARATION TIME **10 MINUTES, PLUS OVERNIGHT SOAKING TIME**
COOKING TIME **2½ HOURS**   SERVES **4**

½ cup dried borlotti beans, or 1 can (14-ounce)
    salt-free borlotti beans in water, drained
    and rinsed

14 ounces vine-ripened tomatoes, cut into quarters

2 tablespoons olive oil

3½ ounces green beans, cut in half

4 tuna steaks

1 handful baby spinach leaves

1 handful arugula

Dressing:

3 tablespoons extra virgin olive oil

1½ tablespoons balsamic vinegar

sea salt and freshly ground black pepper

1   If using dried borlotti beans, place them in a bowl, cover with cold water, and leave to soak overnight or at least 12 hours.

2   The next day, preheat the oven to 275°F. Arrange the tomatoes in a single layer on a baking tray and drizzle with 1½ tablespoons of the olive oil, then roast in the oven 2½ hours, or until dry.

3   Meanwhile, drain the dried beans and rinse thoroughly. Put in a large saucepan, cover with fresh water, and bring to a boil. Boil rapidly 10 minutes, then turn the heat down, cover with a lid, and leave to simmer 1 to 1½ hours until tender; drain thoroughly.

4   Place the green beans in a steamer and steam 1 to 2 minutes until just tender.

5   Preheat the broiler to high. Brush the tuna lightly on both sides with the remaining olive oil, then place on the broiler rack and cook under the hot broiler 2 to 3 minutes on each side. Alternatively, fry in the remaining oil over medium-high heat 2 to 3 minutes on each side.

6   While the tuna is cooking, put the spinach and arugula in a large bowl and mix in the cooked or canned borlotti beans and the green beans. Take the tomatoes out of the oven and add them with their oil. Whisk the dressing ingredients together in a measuring cup or bowl, seasoning lightly, and pour over the salad, mixing until well combined. Serve the tuna with the salad.

stir-fried squid salad

PREPARATION TIME **10 MINUTES**   COOKING TIME **5 MINUTES**   SERVES **4**

2¹/₄ pounds baby squid

2 tablespoons olive oil

1 large fresh red chili, seeded and finely chopped

1 bunch scallions, finely chopped

1 tablespoon Thai fish sauce

3 tablespoons chopped cilantro leaves

3 heaped tablespoons chopped mint leaves

Salad:

4 hearts of lettuce, leaves torn in half

2¹/₂ ounces arugula

1 cucumber, cut into thin strips

1 red bell pepper, seeded and cut into thin strips

Dressing:

6 tablespoons extra virgin olive oil

2 tablespoons lemon juice

1 tablespoon chopped mint leaves

1 tablespoon chopped cilantro leaves

1   To prepare the squid, pull the tentacles out of the sacs and cut them away from the beak part of the head that holds them together. Feel inside each sac for the transparent quill, or backbone, and remove it, then pull off the outer membrane, if present. Finally, rinse the sacs and tentacles under cold running water and pat dry on paper towels. Using a sharp knife, cut down one side of the squid sacs and open out flat. Score the insides with a diamond pattern, then cut into wide strips about 2 inches long; leave the tentacles intact.

2   Place the salad ingredients in a large salad bowl and mix together.

3   Whisk together all the dressing ingredients in a measuring cup or a bowl.

4   Heat the oil in a wok or large skillet over high heat. Add the squid, chili, scallions, and fish sauce and cook, stirring continuously, 2 to 3 minutes until the squid turns a light golden color. Take the wok off the heat and stir in the chopped herbs.

5   Spoon over the prepared salad and cover with the dressing. Serve either warm or cold.

fava bean, pea, smoked tofu, and mint salad

PREPARATION TIME **20 MINUTES**   COOKING TIME **3 TO 4 MINUTES**   SERVES **4**

2¹/₄ pounds fava beans in their pods, shelled
    (2²/₃ cups shelled)

2¹/₄ pounds peas in their pods, shelled
    (3 cups shelled)

5 mint sprigs

5 ounces smoked tofu

Dressing:

3 tablespoons extra virgin olive oil

juice of 1 lime

1 heaped tablespoon chopped mint leaves

sea salt and freshly ground black pepper

1   Place the beans and peas in a steamer. Add the mint sprigs, place over high heat, and cook 3 to 4 minutes until just tender; remove and discard the mint.

2   Rinse the vegetables under cold running water, then drain well and tip into a large salad bowl. Crumble the tofu over the top of the beans and peas.

3   Whisk together the dressing ingredients in a measuring cup or a bowl and season lightly with salt and pepper. Pour over the salad and serve.

oven-roasted butternut squash and beet salad

PREPARATION TIME **15 MINUTES**   COOKING TIME **40 TO 45 MINUTES**   SERVES **4**

2¹/₂ pounds butternut or other squash, peeled,
    seeded, and cut into chunks

3 tablespoons olive oil

1¹/₂ pounds fresh beets, rinsed, peeled, trimmed,
    and cut into quarters

1 cup pine nuts

1 large avocado

¹/₂ tablespoon lemon juice (optional)

5 ounces mixed salad greens, such as lettuce,
    baby leaf spinach, and red chard

2 ounces arugula

Dressing:

6 tablespoons extra virgin olive oil

2 tablespoons balsamic vinegar

salads & sushi

1   Preheat the oven to 350°F. Arrange the pieces of squash on a baking tray and drizzle half of the olive oil over. Repeat with the beet quarters on another tray. Roast the vegetables in the hot oven 40 to 45 minutes, or until tender.

2   Meanwhile, heat a heavy-bottom skillet over medium heat. Add the pine nuts and dry-fry until just starting to turn golden; remove from the heat.

3   Peel the avocado, remove the pit, and slice the flesh. (If you want to prepare the salad earlier, dip the avocado slices into the lemon juice to avoid it turning brown.) Pile the salad greens and arugula into a large salad bowl and mix well. Take the roasted vegetables out of the oven and add to the salad, then top with the avocado slices and pine nuts.

4   Whisk the dressing ingredients together in a measuring cup or a bowl, pour over the salad and serve.

corn fritters with salsa salad

PREPARATION TIME **10 MINUTES**   COOKING TIME **25 TO 30 MINUTES**   MAKES **10**

1 egg white

1¹/₃ cups frozen corn kernels, thawed and drained

¹/₂ fresh red chili, seeded and finely chopped

²/₃ cup sugar-free soymilk

1 egg, beaten

¹/₂ teaspoon sea salt

¹/₂ cup gram flour

1 teaspoon gluten-free baking powder

olive oil for frying

mixed salad greens

Avocado salsa:

1 onion, finely chopped

3 large plum tomatoes, diced

2 avocados, peeled, pitted, and diced

juice of 1 lime

handful chopped cilantro leaves

1   Whisk the egg white in a small bowl, preferably using an electric mixer, until it forms soft peaks. Tip the corn kernels into a large mixing bowl and carefully fold in the whisked egg white, then gently mix in the chili, soymilk, beaten egg, and salt. Sift in the flour and the baking powder and mix thoroughly to form a thick batter.

2   Lightly brush the bottom of a large, heavy-bottom skillet with a little olive oil and place over low heat. Spoon 2 tablespoons of the corn batter into the hot pan to make each fritter; you should be able to fit 3 or 4 in the pan. Fry gently 4 to 5 minutes on each side until golden brown; remove from the pan, drain on kitchen paper, keep warm, and repeat.

3   Meanwhile, mix all the salsa ingredients together in a bowl.

4   Serve the fritters with the salad greens and salsa.

smoked salmon, shrimp, and vegetable sushi

PREPARATION TIME **20 TO 25 MINUTES, PLUS 45 TO 50 MINUTES DRAINING AND COOLING TIME**
COOKING TIME **15 TO 20 MINUTES**   SERVES **4**

2¹/₄ cups sushi rice

4 tablespoons rice vinegar

2 tablespoons fruit sugar

1 teaspoon sea salt

8 sheets toasted nori seaweed,
    each about 8 x 7¹/₄ inches

¹/₄ teaspoon wasabi paste, or to taste

24 to 32 cooked, shelled jumbo shrimp, deveined

9 ounces smoked salmon, cut into strips

2 ripe avocados, peeled, pitted, and thickly
    sliced lengthwise

¹/₂ cucumber, cut lengthwise into thin strips
    ¹/₂ inch wide, seeds discarded

tamari soy sauce for dipping

1   Put the rice in a large mixing bowl and cover with cold water. Swirl the rice around, then drain through a strainer. Repeat until the water stays clear, then leave to drain 30 minutes.

2   Transfer the rice to a large saucepan and pour 1³/₄ cups water over. Bring to a boil over medium heat, then turn the heat down, cover with a lid, clear if possible, and leave to simmer 8 to 10 minutes until all the water is absorbed; with the lid still on, remove from the heat and leave to stand 10 to 15 minutes.

3   Meanwhile, heat the rice vinegar, sugar, and salt in a small saucepan over low heat until all the sugar dissolves; remove from the heat and leave to cool slightly.

4   Spoon the cooked rice into a large, shallow dish. Pour the vinegar mixture over and, with a wooden spatula, gently fold the liquid into the rice; leave to cool completely.

5   Lay a sheet of nori, shiny side down, on a clean cloth. Spread 4 heaped tablespoons of the cold rice over a third of the nori up to the edges. Spread a very thin line of wasabi paste on top. Place 3 or 4 shrimp, 4 or 5 strips salmon (about 1 ounce), 3 slices avocado, and 4 to 6 strips cucumber on the rice in a horizontal line, slightly off-center, nearer the middle of the sheet. Holding the edge of the cloth and the edge of nori nearest to you together, carefully roll the nori over the filling, rolling the cloth with it to secure. Compress the roll slightly so it holds firmly together; repeat with the remaining sheets of nori and filling ingredients.

6   Cut each roll into 5 pieces and serve with a small dish of tamari soy sauce for dipping.

salads & sushi

prosciutto and arugula pizza

PREPARATION TIME **1 HOUR 25 MINUTES**   COOKING TIME **12 TO 15 MINUTES**   SERVES **2**

¹/₂ cup rice flour, plus extra for dusting

³/₄ cup plus 1¹/₂ tablespoons gram flour

3 tablespoons cornmeal

¹/₂ teaspoon salt

1 teaspoon rapid-rise dry yeast

2 tablespoons olive oil

dairy-free margarine for greasing

Topping:

4 tablespoons passata (bottled pureed tomatoes)

1¹/₂ tablespoons tomato paste

5 ounces nitrate-free prosciutto, thinly sliced

2¹/₄ to 3¹/₂ ounces dairy-free cheese, shaved

1 handful arugula

1   Sift the flours, cornmeal, and salt into a large mixing bowl. Add the yeast and mix in well. Make a well in the middle and pour in the oil. Gradually work the flour into the oil, using a wooden spoon or your fingertips, until blended. Pour in 7 tablespoons warm water, a little at a time, and continue mixing to form a soft dough.

2   Turn the dough out onto a surface liberally dusted with rice flour and knead thoroughly about 10 minutes. Place in a clean bowl, cover with a damp cloth, and leave at room temperature 1 hour or until double in size.

3   Heat the oven to 425°F. Grease a baking sheet with dairy-free margarine. Turn the dough out again onto a floured surface and knead about 4 minutes, then form into a ball. Flatten slightly, roll out into a large circle about ½ inch thick and cut with a knife to neaten; transfer to the prepared baking sheet.

4   Make the topping by mixing together the passata and tomato paste in a bowl. Spread this mixture over the pizza crust and top with the prosciutto. Bake in the hot oven 12 to 15 minutes until the crust is starting to brown and the tomato sauce is bubbling. Take the pizza out of the oven, sprinkle the cheese shavings and arugula over the top, and serve.

shrimp and vegetable tempura

PREPARATION TIME **10 MINUTES**   COOKING TIME **30 TO 35 MINUTES**   SERVES **4**

1 zucchini, chopped into 2-inch batons

1¼ pounds butternut or other squash, peeled,
    seeded, and cut into small bite-size chunks

2 red, orange, or yellow bell peppers, seeded and cut
    into wide strips

14 ounces asparagus, woody ends removed, trimmed
    to 2-inch pieces

1 pound cooked, shelled jumbo shrimp, deveined

2 egg yolks, beaten

1⅓ cups plus 2 tablespoons gram flour

¾ cup plus 2½ tablespoons rice flour

1 quart canola or olive oil

tamari soy sauce, for dipping

1   Dry the vegetables as much as possible and drain the shrimp thoroughly.

2   Mix 1 of the egg yolks with ¾ cup ice-cold water in a medium-size mixing bowl. Sift in half
of both flours, then quickly mix with a fork to blend in and make a thick but runny batter,
adding another 1 to 2 tablespoons water if needed. Do not stir too much, as the mixture
should remain a little lumpy. Repeat in another bowl with the other egg and remaining
flours and place this second batch of batter in the refrigerator.

3   Pour the oil into a wok or large saucepan and place over medium-high heat. (To test if the
oil is hot enough, add a little bit of batter to it: If the batter bobs up quickly to the surface
and is sizzling, the oil is ready.)

4   Dip either a piece of vegetable or a shrimp into the batter, shake it a little to remove any
excess batter, and then quickly slip it into the hot oil. Deep-fry the ingredients in batches of
no more than 10 pieces 1 to 3 minutes until lightly golden and cooked through, depending
on the ingredient—the squash will need a little longer than the other vegetables.

5   Lift out with a slotted spoon and drain on paper towels; repeat with the remaining
vegetables and shrimp, using the second batch of batter when the first is used up. Serve
immediately with the tamari soy sauce for dipping.

lunches

thai fishcakes

PREPARATION TIME **10 MINUTES**   COOKING TIME **20 TO 25 MINUTES**
ADDITIONAL TIME **MAKING THE CURRY PASTE**   SERVES **4**

1 pound 2 ounces cod fillets, skinned and any
    remaining bones removed

1 tablespoon Thai fish sauce

1 tablespoon Thai Green Curry Paste (see page 20)

1 large handful chopped cilantro leaves and stems

1 extra-large egg

scant $^1/_2$ cup finely sliced thin green beans

4 scallions, finely sliced

6–8 tablespoons canola or olive oil

Dipping sauce:

1 tablespoon Thai fish sauce

1 tablespoon tamari soy sauce

juice of 1 lime

1 tablespoon chopped cilantro leaves

1   Place the cod, fish sauce, curry paste, cilantro, and egg in a blender or food processor
    and blend thoroughly. Tip into a mixing bowl and stir in the green beans and scallions.

2   Take about 1 tablespoon of the mixture, shape it into a ball with your hands, and place on
    a clean surface, then flatten it slightly with your palm; repeat with the remaining mixture to
    make 12 fishcakes.

3   Heat 2 tablespoons of the oil in a heavy-bottom skillet until hot. Add 3 or 4 of the fishcakes
    and cook over medium heat 3 to 4 minutes on each side until golden and crisp; remove with
    a pancake turner, drain on paper towels, and keep warm. Repeat with the other fishcakes,
    adding more oil to the pan each time.

4   Meanwhile, mix all the dipping sauce ingredients together in a small serving bowl.

5   Serve the fishcakes with the dipping sauce and mixed salad greens.

light lunches

spaghetti vongole

PREPARATION TIME **5 MINUTES**   COOKING TIME **10 MINUTES**   SERVES **4**

4¹/₂ pounds fresh clams in their shells

3 tablespoons olive oil

14 ounces gluten-free spaghetti, or other gluten-free pasta shape

4 garlic cloves, chopped

scant 1¹/₂ cups organic dry white wine

2 large handfuls flat-leaf parsley, coarsely chopped

sea salt and freshly ground black pepper

1   Wash the clams thoroughly under cold running water, discarding any that are open or have cracked shells.

2   Bring a large saucepan of water to a boil. Add 1 tablespoon of the oil, then the spaghetti, pushing it down into the water as it softens. Cook over medium heat 8 to 10 minutes, or according to the package directions, stirring frequently to make sure the spaghetti doesn't stick together.

3   Meanwhile, heat the remaining oil in a large, heavy-bottom saucepan. Add the garlic and clams, cover the pan with a lid, and leave to cook over medium heat 3 minutes. Pour in the wine, cover the pan, and cook 2 to 3 minutes until the clams open; remove from the heat and discard any clams that have not opened. Stir in the chopped parsley and season lightly with salt and pepper.

4   Drain the spaghetti and rinse well with boiling water, then drain again. Tip into the pan of hot clams, stir to combine, and serve immediately.

light lunches

lunches

kedgeree

PREPARATION TIME **10 MINUTES**   COOKING TIME **30 TO 35 MINUTES**   SERVES **4**

1½ pounds undyed smoked haddock fillets

7 tablespoons dairy-free margarine

1 onion, finely chopped

½ tablespoon paprika

heaped 1¾ cups long-grain rice, rinsed

2 handfuls chopped flat-leaf parsley

3 hard-boiled eggs, shelled and chopped

sea salt and freshly ground black pepper

1 Put the haddock fillets in a heavy-bottom saucepan, cover with 4 cups boiling water, then with a lid, and simmer gently about 10 minutes. Lift the fish out of the pan with a slotted spatula, place it on a plate, and remove and discard any skin and bones. Flake the flesh with a fork. Strain and reserve the cooking liquid.

2 Melt the margarine in a large, heavy-bottom pan. Add the onion and cook over medium heat 2 to 3 minutes until starting to turn golden. Add the paprika and rice, then stir in the reserved cooking liquid from the haddock. Cover with a lid and bring to a boil, then turn the heat down, and leave to simmer 15 to 20 minutes until the rice is cooked, topping up with extra boiling water if it is all absorbed.

3 Stir in the flaked fish and chopped parsley and continue cooking, uncovered, until all the liquid is absorbed; season lightly with salt and pepper. Serve with the chopped eggs on top.

tomato, basil, and olive penne

PREPARATION TIME **5 MINUTES**   COOKING TIME **1 HOUR**   SERVES **4**

16 large vine-ripened tomatoes,
    about 4 pounds total weight
4½ tablespoons olive oil
1 large onion, chopped
2 large garlic cloves, chopped

heaped 1 cup pitted black olives cut in half
14 ounces gluten-free penne, or other gluten-free
    pasta shape
4 heaped tablespoons chopped basil leaves
sea salt and freshly ground black pepper

1   Preheat the oven to 350°F. With a sharp knife, cut a cross in the skin of each tomato, then place on a baking tray. Drizzle with 2½ tablespoons of the olive oil and bake in the hot oven 45 minutes.

2   Five minutes before the tomatoes are ready, heat 1 tablespoon of the oil in a heavy-bottom saucepan. Add the onion and cook over medium heat 2 to 3 minutes until starting to turn golden.

3   Take the tomatoes out of the oven, remove the skins with a knife and fork, and gently break up the flesh. Add the garlic to the saucepan and fry 30 seconds, then stir in the tomato flesh along with any juices. Add the olives and season lightly with salt and pepper. Cook 12 to 14 minutes until the sauce reduces by about a half and is runny, but still thick.

4   Meanwhile, bring a large saucepan of water to a boil. Add the remaining oil, then the pasta, and cook over medium heat 8 to 10 minutes, or according to the package directions, stirring frequently to make sure the pasta doesn't stick together; drain and rinse well with boiling water, then drain again. Tip the pasta into a large serving bowl.

5   Stir the basil into the sauce, spoon over the pasta and serve.

asparagus frittata

PREPARATION TIME **5 MINUTES**   COOKING TIME **7 TO 10 MINUTES**   SERVES **2**

light lunches

12 asparagus spears, woody ends removed

6 eggs

1 tablespoon dairy-free margarine

¹/₄ cup finely diced silken tofu

4 scallions, finely chopped

1 tablespoon chopped mint leaves

1 tablespoon chopped dill

sea salt and freshly ground black pepper

1   Place the asparagus in a steamer and cook over medium heat 3 to 4 minutes until just tender but still slightly crunchy; drain.

2   Meanwhile, beat the eggs thoroughly in a mixing bowl and add a little salt and pepper.

3   Preheat the broiler to high. Melt the margarine in a heavy-bottom skillet with an ovenproof handle over low heat. Pour the egg mixture into the pan and swirl it around so it covers the bottom of the pan. Quickly top with the tofu, scallions, and herbs, distributing them evenly. Finally, arrange the asparagus spears on top.

4   Cook the frittata on the stovetop 3 to 4 minutes until golden on the bottom, then place the skillet under the hot broiler 1 to 2 minutes until the egg mixture is cooked through and the top of the frittata is golden; remove from the pan and place on a serving plate. Serve warm or cool, with mixed salad greens.

spinach tart

PREPARATION TIME **15 MINUTES PLUS 30 MINUTES CHILLING TIME**   COOKING TIME **40 TO 50 MINUTES**
ADDITIONAL TIME **MAKING THE PASTRY DOUGH**   SERVES **4**

dairy-free margarine for greasing

1 recipe quantity Rich Piecrust Dough,
    or gluten-free version (see page 21)

rice flour for dusting

1 tablespoon olive oil

9 ounces baby leaf spinach

2¹/₂ ounces tofu

2 extra-large eggs plus 5 extra-large egg yolks

6 tablespoons sugar-free soymilk

¹/₂ teaspoon freshly grated nutmeg

sea salt and freshly ground black pepper

lunches

1   Preheat the oven to 400°F. Grease a 10-inch tart pan, 1¹/₄ inches deep, with dairy-free
    margarine.

2   Roll out the dough on a board liberally dusted with rice flour into a circle about ¹/₈ inch
    thick and 1¹/₄ inches larger all around than the tart pan, to allow enough dough for the
    sides. Be careful, as the dough will still be slightly sticky. Neaten the edge with a knife,
    then ease the dough into the pan, pressing down carefully to remove any air pockets. If
    the dough looks too fragile to lift into the pan, simply place the pan face down on top of
    the dough and trim around to neaten it, allowing extra dough for the sides, then invert the
    board to drop the dough into the pan.

3   Line the tart shell with a piece of baking parchment and cover with baking beans. Bake in
    the hot oven 10 to 12 minutes until just golden. Take the tart shell out of the oven and turn
    the oven down to 350°F.

4   Gently heat the olive oil in a large saucepan or wok. Add the spinach and cook over very
    low heat 2 to 3 minutes until it just wilts, turning all the time. Spread the spinach over the
    prepared tart shell, then crumble the tofu over the top. Whisk the eggs, egg yolks, soymilk,
    and nutmeg together in a bowl, then season lightly with salt and pepper. Pour this mixture
    over the spinach and tofu in the tart shell.

5   Bake in the hot oven 30 to 35 minutes until the filling is cooked through. Take the tart out of
    the oven and leave to cool in the pan until the filling has set, then carefully ease out onto a
    plate. Serve with mixed salad greens.

asparagus, oyster mushroom, and sugar-snap stir-fry

PREPARATION TIME **5 MINUTES**   COOKING TIME **6 TO 7 MINUTES**   SERVES **4**

light lunches

1 tablespoon olive oil

1 tablespoon sesame oil

2 bunches scallions, finely sliced

1-inch piece fresh gingerroot, peeled and finely chopped

$^1/_2$ large fresh red chili, seeded and finely chopped

2 garlic cloves, chopped

1 pound 2 ounces fresh asparagus, woody ends
   removed, cut in half lengthwise

10 ounces sugar-snap peas

9 ounces oyster mushrooms, cut into
   bite-size pieces

3 tablespoons tamari soy sauce

$^1/_2$ cup toasted sesame seeds

2 handfuls chopped cilantro leaves

1 handful chopped mint leaves

1 Heat both the oils in a wok over high heat. Add the scallions and cook, stirring continuously, 1 minute. Toss in the ginger, chili, and garlic, then stir in the asparagus and cook, stirring continuously, 1 minute.

2 Add the sugar-snap peas and mushrooms and leave to cook 1 minute. Add the tamari soy sauce and stir-fry 3 to 4 minutes until all the vegetables are cooked through but remain slightly crunchy.

3 Stir in the sesame seeds and the chopped herbs. Check the seasoning and add extra tamari soy sauce, if needed. Serve with steamed basmati rice or rice noodles.

snacks

The great news is that you don't have to go without biscuits, brownies, cookies, cakes, or tartlets. There are wonderful alternative ingredients that you can use, including soy products, rice and gram flour, and ground almonds. And here you'll find a mouth-watering collection of recipes using these ingredients. Baking is pure comfort food—in the making as well as the eating. All you need are a few baking trays, some ingredients, and a little bit of time. Most of the recipes in this chapter will keep for a few days, so you can make them on the weekend and munch through them during the week. Whether it's rich Chocolate and Hazlenut Brownies, tangy Lemon Polenta Cake, creamy Fruit Tartlets, or crunchy Sunflower Seed Crackers, here are gorgeous treats for you to enjoy and, if they really insist, to share with family and friends!

chocolate and hazlenut brownies

PREPARATION TIME **10 MINUTES**   COOKING TIME **12 TO 15 MINUTES**   MAKES **20**

5 ounces dairy-free margarine,
    plus extra for greasing
7 ounces dairy-free dark chocolate,
    with at least 70 percent cocoa solids
1 cup fruit sugar
2 extra-large eggs, beaten

1 teaspoon vanilla extract
$^1/_4$ cup plus 1 tablespoon rice flour
4 tablespoons gram flour
1 teaspoon gluten-free baking powder
heaped $^3/_4$ cup chopped hazelnuts

1   Preheat the oven to 350°F. Grease an 8- x 12-inch baking pan with dairy-free margarine
    and line the bottom with baking parchment.

2   Break the chocolate into small pieces and place in a large heatproof bowl. Rest the bowl
    over a pan of gently simmering water, making sure the bottom of the bowl does not touch
    the water; stir from time to time until the chocolate has melted. Add the margarine to the
    bowl and continue stirring occasionally until it is completely melted and blended with
    the chocolate.

3   Remove the bowl from the heat and stir in the sugar, followed by the beaten eggs and
    vanilla extract. Stir to mix well, then sift the flours and baking powder into the bowl and
    carefully fold in with a metal spoon, making sure the batter is thoroughly combined, but
    not stirred too heavily, or the air will be lost; fold in the nuts.

4   Spoon the batter into the prepared pan, spreading it evenly into the corners with the back
    of the spoon. Bake in the hot oven 12 to 15 minutes until risen and firm to the touch and a
    skewer inserted in the middle has just a little brownie sticking to it. Remove from the oven
    and leave to cool in the pan 5 minutes, then transfer to a wire rack and leave to cool
    completely. Cut into 20 squares.

cookies & brownies

fig and pecan nut crunchies

PREPARATION TIME **10 MINUTES**   COOKING TIME **20 TO 22 MINUTES**   MAKES **10**

5 ounces dairy-free margarine,
　　plus extra for greasing

scant ¹/₃ cup fruit sugar

1 tablespoon honey

1 teaspoon freshly grated nutmeg

4 tablespoons barley flour

10 tablespoons gram flour

¹/₃ cup rice flour

1 teaspoon baking powder

1¹/₂ cups jumbo rolled oats

1 cup chopped sugar-free dried figs

scant ¹/₂ cup chopped pecans

1   Preheat the oven to 350°F and lightly grease a cookie sheet with dairy-free margarine.
    Place the margarine, sugar, and honey in a heavy-bottom saucepan and heat gently until
    the margarine melts and the sugar dissolves; stir in the nutmeg.

2   Sift the flours with the baking powder into a large mixing bowl. Add the oats, figs, and
    pecans and mix well. Pour in the melted margarine mixture and mix together thoroughly.

3   Take 2 tablespoons of the dough and shape into a ball with your hands. Place on the
    prepared cookie sheet, spaced well apart. Repeat until you have used all the dough, then
    flatten each ball slightly with the palm of your hand.

4   Bake in the hot oven 20 to 22 minutes until golden brown. Take the crunchies out of the
    oven, transfer to a wire rack, and leave to cool completely.

almond cookies

PREPARATION TIME **10 MINUTES**   COOKING TIME **14 TO 17 MINUTES**   MAKES **14 TO 16**

6 ounces dairy-free margarine

4 tablespoons fruit sugar

³/₄ cup plus 1 tablespoon rice flour

¹/₃ cup plus 1 tablespoon gram flour

¹/₃ cup finely ground blanched almonds

scant ¹/₂ teaspoon almond extract

1 Preheat the oven to 350°F. Line two cookie sheets with baking parchment.

2 Place the margarine and sugar in a heavy-bottom saucepan and heat gently until the margarine has melted and the sugar has dissolved. Bring to a boil, then turn the heat down and leave to simmer 4 to 5 minutes until the mixture caramelizes slightly and becomes syrupy.

3 Sift the flours and ground almonds into a large mixing bowl. Pour in the sugar mixture, add the almond extract, and stir thoroughly with a wooden spoon until mixed.

4 Spoon the dough, 1 tablespoon at a time, onto the prepared cookie sheets to form 14 to 16 balls. Press down on each ball with the back of the spoon to make a cookie shape.

5 Bake in the hot oven 10 to 12 minutes until light brown. Take the cookies out of the oven and leave to cool 5 minutes, then transfer to a wire rack and leave to cool completely.

lemon polenta cake

PREPARATION TIME **10 MINUTES**   COOKING TIME **35 TO 40 MINUTES**   SERVES **10**

10 ounces dairy-free margarine, softened,
    plus extra for greasing

1 cup fruit sugar

4 extra-large eggs, beaten

4 tablespoons honey

heaped 2$^1/_3$ cups quick-cook polenta

1 cup finely ground blanched almonds, plus extra
    for topping

1 teaspoon gluten-free baking powder

juice of 1$^1/_2$ lemons and grated zest of 1 lemon, plus
    pared or grated zest of another lemon to decorate

1   Preheat the oven to 350°F. Lightly grease a deep 8-inch springform cake pan with dairy-free margarine and line the bottom with a circle of baking parchment.

2   Using an electric mixer, beat the margarine and sugar together in a large mixing bowl until light and fluffy. Gradually beat in the eggs, a little at a time, then the honey.

3   Using a metal spoon, fold in the polenta, ground almonds, and baking powder, then the lemon juice and zest. Mix thoroughly and pour the batter into the prepared cake pan.

4   Bake in the hot oven 35 to 40 minutes until golden brown around the side and firm to the touch, and a skewer inserted in the middle comes out clean; you will notice cracks all over the top. Take the cake out of the oven, leave to cool in the pan 5 minutes, then turn out onto a wire rack and leave to cool completely.

5   Sprinkle with the extra ground almonds and the pared or grated lemon zest.

spicy gingerbread

PREPARATION TIME **10 MINUTES**   COOKING TIME **20 TO 25 MINUTES**   SERVES **8**

7 tablespoons dairy-free margarine,
    softened, plus extra for greasing
scant $^1/_2$ cup fruit sugar
1 egg, beaten
3 tablespoons date syrup
$^1/_2$ cup plus 1$^1/_2$ tablespoons rice flour

$^1/_2$ cup gram flour
scant $^1/_3$ cup millet flour
2 teaspoons ground ginger
$^3/_4$-inch piece fresh gingerroot, peeled and
    finely chopped

1   Preheat the oven to 350°F. Lightly grease an 8-inch springform cake pan with dairy-free margarine and line the bottom with a circle of baking parchment.

2   Using an electric mixer, beat the margarine and sugar together in a large mixing bowl until light and fluffy. Gradually beat in the egg, a little at a time, then the date syrup.

3   Sift in the flours and add the ground ginger and the fresh gingerroot. Fold in with a metal spoon until the batter is thoroughly mixed.

4   Pour the batter into the prepared pan and bake in the hot oven 20 to 25 minutes until it is a rich golden brown and a skewer inserted into the middle comes out with just a little of the batter sticking to it. Take the gingerbread out of the oven, leave to cool in the pan 3 to 4 minutes, then turn out onto a wire rack and leave to cool completely before serving.

banana bread

PREPARATION TIME **10 MINUTES**　　COOKING TIME **45 TO 50 MINUTES**　　SERVES **6**

cakes

7 tablespoons dairy-free margarine, softened,
　　plus extra for greasing

scant $^2/_3$ cup fruit sugar

2 extra-large eggs

1 teaspoon vanilla extract

$^1/_3$ cup plus 2 tablespoons rice flour

scant $^1/_4$ cup millet flour

$^1/_3$ cup plus 1 tablespoon gram flour

2 teaspoons gluten-free baking powder

4 very ripe bananas, mashed

1　Preheat the oven to 350°F. Grease a 9- x 5-inch bread pan with dairy-free margarine.

2　Using an electric mixer, beat the margarine and sugar together in a large mixing bowl until light and fluffy. Gradually beat in the eggs, a little at a time, then the vanilla extract.

3　Sift the flours and baking powder into a clean bowl. With a metal spoon, carefully fold half the flour into the mixture, then repeat with the remaining flour. Add the bananas and fold in until thoroughly mixed in.

4　Spoon the batter into the prepared pan and bake in the hot oven 45 to 50 minutes until a rich golden brown on top and firm to the touch. When the banana bread is cooked, a skewer inserted in the middle should come out with just a little of the batter sticking to it. Take the banana bread out of the oven, leave to cool in the pan 3 to 4 minutes, then turn out onto a wire rack and leave to cool completely before serving.

carrot and beet cupcakes

PREPARATION TIME **10 MINUTES**   COOKING TIME **15 TO 20 MINUTES**   MAKES **10**

5 ounces dairy-free margarine, softened

²/₃ cup fruit sugar

3 eggs, beaten

¹/₃ cup plus 1¹/₂ tablespoons rice flour

²/₃ cup gram flour

1 teaspoon gluten-free baking powder

1 teaspoon baking soda

1 teaspoon ground cinnamon

scant 2 cups peeled and grated carrots

1 cup peeled and grated fresh beets

Topping:

7 tablespoons soy yogurt

2 tablespoons honey

1   Preheat the oven to 350°F. Arrange 10 paper muffin liners in a muffin pan.

2   Using an electric mixer, beat the margarine and sugar together in a large mixing bowl
    until light and fluffy. Gradually beat in the eggs, a little at a time, until well mixed.

3   Sift the flours, baking powder, baking soda, and ground cinnamon into the mixture, then
    quickly fold it in, followed by the grated carrots and beets, using a metal spoon. Make sure
    the batter is well blended, but take care not to overmix.

4   Divide the batter into the muffin liners and bake in the hot oven 10 minutes, then cover
    them with a sheet of baking parchment to prevent them from overbrowning and bake 5 to
    10 minutes longer until well risen and a skewer inserted in the middle comes out clean.
    Take the cupcakes out of the oven, transfer to a wire rack, and leave to cool completely.

5   When the cupcakes are cool, prepare the topping. Using a whisk or electric mixer, whisk
    together the yogurt and honey in a bowl until smooth; spread a little of the topping over
    each cupcake.

apricot, mango, and coconut bars

PREPARATION TIME **10 MINUTES**   COOKING TIME **45 TO 50 MINUTES**   MAKES **10**

dairy-free margarine for greasing

³/₄ cup finely chopped sugar-free dried
    unsulfured apricots

³/₄ cup finely chopped sugar-free dried mango

³/₄ cup unsweetened coconut flakes

7 ounces creamed coconut

2 cups oatmeal

2 tablespoons olive oil

4 tablespoons mango or date syrup

1   Preheat the oven to 350°F. Grease an 8- x 12-inch baking pan with dairy-free margarine
    and line the base with baking parchment.

2   Put the dried apricots and mango in a heavy-bottom saucepan with 2 cups water. Bring to
    a boil, then turn the heat down and leave to simmer 15 to 20 minutes until the fruit softens
    and the water is absorbed.

3   Meanwhile, heat a heavy-bottom skillet over medium heat until hot. Toss in the coconut
    flakes and dry-fry until light brown, turning frequently to prevent burning. Tip the coconut
    into a bowl. Melt the creamed coconut in a small, heavy-bottom saucepan over very low
    heat.

4   Place the oatmeal in a large mixing bowl and make a well in the middle. Pour in the oil and
    work it into the oatmeal with your fingertips, making sure the oil is evenly distributed. Stir
    in the melted creamed coconut, the mango or date syrup, and half the soft apricot and
    mango mixture, mixing thoroughly.

5   Spread half the oatmeal mixture in a thin layer over the bottom of the prepared baking pan,
    pressing down firmly with your fingertips or the back of a metal spoon. Spread the remain-
    ing apricot and mango mixture over the top, then spread the remaining oat mixture on top.

6   Bake in the hot oven 25 to 30 minutes until golden brown and firm. Remove the pan from the
    oven, sprinkle the coconut flakes over the top, and leave to cool in the tin 3 to 4 minutes. Cut
    into 10 bars, remove from the pan, and leave to cool completely on a wire rack before serving.

raspberry tartlets

PREPARATION TIME **15 MINUTES**   COOKING TIME **35 TO 40 MINUTES**
ADDITIONAL TIME **MAKING THE PASTRY DOUGH**   MAKES **6**

6 tablespoons dairy-free margarine, softened,
   plus extra for greasing
1 recipe quantity Sweet Rich Piecrust Dough
   (see page 22)
rice flour for dusting

¹/₄ cup fruit sugar, plus extra for dusting
1 extra-large egg, beaten
1 cup finely ground blanched almonds
7 ounces fresh raspberries

1 Preheat the oven to 375°F. Grease a six-hole muffin tray with dairy-free margarine.
2 Gently roll out the dough on a surface liberally dusted with rice flour until about ¹/₈ inch thick. Using a biscuit cutter that is slightly larger in diameter than the muffin holes, cut out 6 dough circles; be very gentle, as the dough will still be slightly sticky.
3 Lift the dough circles into the tray (you might need to use a metal spatula) and press down lightly to remove any air pockets. Line each tartlet shell with a piece of baking parchment and cover with baking beans. Bake in the hot oven 8 to 10 minutes until firm and light golden.
4 Meanwhile, using an electric mixer, beat the margarine and sugar together in a large mixing bowl until light and fluffy. Gradually beat in the egg, a little at a time, until well mixed, then fold in the ground almonds.
5 Take the tartlet shells out of the oven and remove the parchment and beans. Spoon the prepared filling mixture into the tartlet shells. Press a small handful of raspberries into each tartlet and return to the hot oven 25 to 30 minutes until firm and golden brown. Take the tartlets out of the oven, leave to cool in the tray 5 minutes, then transfer to a wire rack to cool completely. Grind the extra sugar with a stick blender attachment or using a mortar and pestle and sprinkle over the tartlets before serving.

fruit tartlets

PREPARATION TIME **20 MINUTES**   COOKING TIME **25 MINUTES**
ADDITIONAL TIME **MAKING THE PASTRY DOUGH**   MAKES **4**

dairy-free margarine for greasing

1 recipe quantity Sweet Rich Piecrust Dough

   (see page 22)

rice flour for dusting

1 cup soymilk

1¹/₂ teaspoons cornstarch

3 extra-large egg yolks

3¹/₂ tbsp fruit sugar

¹/₂ teaspoon vanilla extract

9 to 15 strawberries, depending on size, hulled and cut

   in half, or 3 peaches or nectarines, peeled, pitted,

   and sliced lengthwise into eight pieces

1 tablespoon sugar-free apricot jam

1 Preheat the oven to 400°F. Grease four 5-inch tartlet pans with removable bottoms, ³/₄ inch deep, with dairy-free margarine.

2 Gently roll out the dough on a surface liberally dusted with rice flour until about ¹/₈ inch thick. Using a biscuit cutter that is slightly larger in diameter than the pans, to allow enough dough for the sides, cut out 4 dough circles, discarding any extra dough; be very gentle, as the dough will still be slightly sticky.

3 Lift the dough circles into each pan (you might need to use a metal spatula) and press down lightly to remove any air pockets. Line each tartlet shell with a piece of baking parchment and cover with baking beans. Place the tartlet pans on a baking tray. Bake in the hot oven 8 to 10 minutes until firm and light golden.

4 Meanwhile, heat the soymilk in a heavy-bottom saucepan over low heat until almost boiling. In a small bowl, stir 1 teaspoon water into the cornstarch. Whisk the egg yolks in a large bowl 2 minutes, then add the sugar and the cornstarch mixture and whisk 2 to 3 minutes longer until thick. Pour in the warm milk and add the vanilla extract, stirring well. Pour the sauce back into the pan and heat gently 5 to 10 minutes, stirring or whisking, until thick and creamy.

5 Take the tartlet shells out of the oven and remove the parchment and beans. Turn the oven down to 350°F. Divide the custard between the shells, arrange 3 to 5 strawberry halves or 4 peach or nectarine slices on each one and bake 15 minutes. Take the tartlets out of the oven and leave to cool, then remove from the pans.

6 Gently heat the apricot jam with about 1 teaspoon water in a small saucepan until the jam dissolves. Brush the tops of the fruit lightly with this glaze, using a pastry brush, and serve.

tartlets

sunflower seed crackers

PREPARATION TIME **10 MINUTES**   COOKING TIME **30 MINUTES**   MAKES **8**

snacks

4 tablespoons dairy-free margarine,
  plus extra for greasing
scant $\frac{1}{2}$ cup sunflower seeds
2 cups gram flour

1$\frac{1}{4}$ cups rice flour, plus extra for dusting
1$\frac{1}{2}$ teaspoons gluten-free baking powder
$\frac{1}{2}$ teaspoon salt
3 tablespoons olive oil

1 Preheat the oven to 350°F. Grease two cookie sheets with dairy-free margarine.

2 Place the sunflower seeds in a heavy-bottom skillet over medium heat and dry-fry until just beginning to brown; remove from the pan.

3 Sift the flours, baking powder, and salt into a large mixing bowl. Make a well in the middle and pour in the oil. With your fingertips, rub the oil into the flour mixture. Add the margarine and, using your fingertips, rub in until thoroughly mixed. Stir in the toasted sunflower seeds.

4 Make a well in the flour mixture and pour in $\frac{2}{3}$ cup water. Gradually mix in until well blended. Bring together to form a ball of soft dough.

5 Turn out the dough onto a surface liberally dusted with rice flour and roll out the dough with a rolling pin until about $\frac{1}{4}$ inch thick. Using a 5-inch biscuit cutter, cut out 8 circles of dough. You'll need to keep shaping the dough into a ball and then rolling it out again in order to cut all the circles. Place on the prepared cookie sheets and bake in the hot oven 28 to 30 minutes until golden brown.

6 Take the crackers out of the oven, leave to cool on the sheets 3 to 4 minutes, then transfer to a wire rack and leave to cool completely before serving with dairy-free cheese, Avocado Salsa (see page 64), or Smoked Salmon Pâté (see page 42).

sun-dried tomato oatcakes

PREPARATION TIME **10 MINUTES**   COOKING TIME **20 TO 25 MINUTES**   MAKES **8**

2 tablespoons dairy-free margarine,
   plus extra for greasing
2 cups ground rolled oats
$^1/_2$ teaspoon baking soda

$^1/_2$ teaspoon dried oregano
5 tablespoons drained and chopped sun-dried
   tomatoes in oil

crackers

1 Preheat the oven to 400°F. Grease eight 5-inch tartlet pans with removable bottoms, $^3/_4$ inch deep, with dairy-free margarine.

2 Mix together the oats, baking soda, and oregano in a large mixing bowl and make a well in the middle. Melt the margarine in a saucepan over low heat and pour into the well. With a wooden spoon, gradually mix the melted margarine into the oat mixture, making sure it is evenly distributed. Add the sun-dried tomatoes and 7 tablespoons water and mix until well combined.

3 Divide the dough into 8 portions and press one portion into the bottom of each prepared tartlet pan. You may find the back of a metal spoon works better than your fingers, as the mixture is quite sticky. Place the tartlet pans on a baking tray.

4 Bake in the hot oven 20 to 25 minutes until golden brown. Take the oatcakes out of the oven and leave to cool in the pans 5 minutes, then turn out onto a wire rack and leave to cool completely before serving with dairy-free cheese, hummus or Artichoke Pâté (see page 45).

dinners

If you thought you couldn't have risotto, pasta, or curry any longer,

think again. This chapter is packed with mouth-watering main courses,

many of which you'll be amazed to find you can eat. Delicious Gnocchi

with Mushroom and Pancetta Sauce provides a substantial, warming meal,

and Salmon Fishcakes, with their crunchy coating, will be a hit with your

kids. Choose from a range of quick suppers that can be whipped up in less

than 30 minutes, such as Pork with Chestnuts, Apple, and Sage; much-

loved family favorites, such as Spaghetti with Meatballs; or indulgent meals

for a special occasion, such as Duck with Cherry and Juniper Sauce or

Herbed Monkfish Wrapped in Prosciutto. This is food for everyone—for

sharing good times together.

chicken farci with pea and mint puree

PREPARATION TIME **10 MINUTES, PLUS 2 HOURS MARINATING TIME**   COOKING TIME **35 MINUTES**
ADDITIONAL TIME **MAKING THE STOCK**   SERVES **4**

4 skinless, boneless chicken breast halves

$^1/_2$ cup olive oil

juice of 1 lime

2 shallots, finely chopped

1 pound 2 ounces peas in their pods, shelled
   ($1^1/_3$ cups shelled)

$^3/_4$ cup Vegetable Stock (see page 25),
   or stock made from gluten-, yeast-,
   and dairy-free bouillon powder

2 heaped tablespoons chopped mint leaves

2 tablespoons chopped silken tofu

sea salt and freshly ground black pepper

poultry

1   Arrange the chicken pieces in a large nonmetallic dish. Mix 6 tablespoons of the oil with the lime juice in a small measuring cup, then pour over the chicken; cover and leave in the refrigerator to marinate 2 hours.

2   Preheat the oven to 350°F. Heat the remaining oil in a heavy-bottom saucepan. Add the shallots and fry over low heat 1 to 2 minutes. Add the peas and stock and cook 5 minutes. Stir in the mint, then season lightly with salt and pepper.

3   Add the tofu to the saucepan, then blend with an electric mixer. Alternatively, blend the mixture in a blender or food processor. Pour the mixture into a strainer set over a bowl and work it through with a wooden spoon to form a puree, reserving the liquid.

4   Remove the chicken from the dish, discarding the marinade. Make a long horizontal slit through the thickest part of each piece without cutting right through, to create a pocket. Stuff as much puree as you can into each pocket, then close up the opening with wooden toothpicks.

5   Arrange the stuffed chicken pieces in a baking dish and spread a thin layer of the remaining puree over the top of each. Pour the reserved liquid onto the bottom of the dish, taking care not to pour it onto the chicken. Bake in the hot oven 25 minutes, or until the chicken is cooked through and the juices run clear. Remove the toothpicks and serve with boiled new potatoes and vegetables.

chicken and herb risotto

PREPARATION TIME **5 MINUTES**   COOKING TIME **25 TO 30 MINUTES**
ADDITIONAL TIME **MAKING THE STOCK**   SERVES **4**

3^1/$_3$ cups Chicken or Vegetable Stock
    (see pages 24–5), or vegetable stock made from
    gluten-, yeast-, and dairy-free bouillon powder
6 tablespoons olive oil
4 skinless, boneless chicken breast halves,
    cut into bite-size pieces
1 small onion, finely chopped

2 tablespoons chopped flat-leaf parsley
2 tablespoons chopped mint leaves
2 tablespoons chopped basil leaves
scant 1^1/$_4$ cups arborio or other risotto rice
scant 1^1/$_4$ cups organic dry white wine
sea salt and freshly ground black pepper

1 Heat the stock in a saucepan until almost boiling, then turn the heat down, cover with a lid, and leave to simmer while you prepare the rice mixture.

2 Heat 2 tablespoons of the oil in a large, heavy-bottom saucepan. Add the chicken pieces and cook over medium heat 5 to 6 minutes until light brown; remove from the pan with a slotted spoon and leave to one side.

3 Put the remaining oil in the pan and heat until hot. Add the onion and cook over medium heat 2 to 3 minutes until starting to turn golden, then stir in half of the chopped herbs. Add the rice and stir thoroughly so each grain is coated with oil.

4 Pour a little of the wine into the mixture and stir. Continue cooking over low heat, gradually adding and stirring in the wine until it is all absorbed. Add the chicken and a ladleful of the simmering stock and stir until all the liquid is absorbed. Continue adding stock and stirring 18 to 20 minutes until the rice is just tender, but still has a little bite and all the liquid is absorbed.

5 Stir in the remaining herbs and season lightly with salt and pepper. Serve with mixed salad leaves.

chicken with salsa verde

PREPARATION TIME **10 MINUTES**   COOKING TIME **10 TO 12 MINUTES**   SERVES **4**

1 tablespoon olive oil

4 skinless, boneless chicken breast halves

12 ounces green beans, topped and tailed

2 bags (10-ounce) baby leaf spinach

Salsa verde:

2 heaped tablespoons chopped basil leaves

2 heaped tablespoons chopped mint leaves

2 heaped tablespoons chopped flat-leaf parsley

1 garlic clove, coarsely chopped

6 anchovies in oil, drained and chopped

2 tablespoons capers in brine, rinsed

juice of $1/2$ lemon

2 tablespoons olive oil

poultry

1   Make the salsa verde by putting the herbs, garlic, anchovies, and capers into a food processor and blending to form a paste. With the motor running, gradually pour in the lemon juice and the oil until well combined; transfer to a bowl and cover.

2   Heat the oil in a large, heavy-bottom saucepan. Add the chicken pieces, cover with a lid, and cook over medium heat, turning occasionally, 10 to 12 minutes until cooked through and the juices run clear.

3   About halfway through the cooking time, place the beans in a steamer and steam 2 minutes. Add the spinach and continue steaming 1 minute until the beans are just tender and the spinach is beginning to wilt.

4   Spread the salsa verde over the chicken pieces and serve with the beans and spinach and with fried or broiled slices of Quick Polenta (see page 143) and mixed salad greens.

thai-style green chicken curry

PREPARATION TIME **10 MINUTES**   COOKING TIME **20 TO 25 MINUTES**
ADDITIONAL TIME **MAKING THE CURRY PASTE**   SERVES **4**

poultry

2 tablespoons olive oil

4 skinless, boneless chicken breast halves,
    cut into thin strips

1²/₃ cups coconut milk

2 tablespoons Thai Green Curry Paste (see page 20)

3 tablespoons Thai fish sauce

4 kaffir lime leaves, or a strip of lime peel

4 ounces green beans, topped

1 red or yellow bell pepper, seeded and cut into
    thin strips

4 ounces sugar-snap peas

4 ounces beansprouts

1 small handful sweet basil leaves, cut in half

¹/₂ large fresh green chili, seeded and cut into
    fine strips

1 large handful cilantro leaves

1 Heat a wok until hot, pour in the oil, and swirl it around. Add the chicken and cook over medium heat, stirring continuously, 2 to 3 minutes until light brown; remove and put on a plate. Pour the coconut milk into the wok and cook gently 4 to 5 minutes. Add the curry paste and cook 2 to 3 minutes, stirring well.

2 Add the fish sauce, lime leaves or strip of lime peel, green beans, and bell pepper to the wok and cook gently 3 to 4 minutes; do not let it boil or the coconut milk will curdle. Add the sugar-snap peas and beansprouts and cook 10 minutes until the chicken is cooked through and the juices run clear.

3 Check the seasoning and add a little more fish sauce, if desired. Sprinkle with the basil, chili, and cilantro and serve with steamed basmati rice.

tender roast chicken

PREPARATION TIME **10 MINUTES**   COOKING TIME **1¾ HOURS**
ADDITIONAL TIME **MAKING THE STOCK**   SERVES **4**

4-pound chicken, oven-ready

1 tablespoon olive oil

1 large garlic clove, sliced

4 rosemary sprigs

1³/₄ pounds potatoes, peeled and cut into quarters

1 cup Chicken or Vegetable Stock (see pages 24–5),
    or vegetable stock made from gluten-, yeast-,
    and dairy-free bouillon powder

1 cup organic dry white wine

sea salt and freshly ground black pepper

1   Preheat the oven to 350°F. Place the chicken in a large baking dish with a lid and rub
with the oil. With a sharp knife, make incisions in the flesh along the breast and top of the
thighs. Insert a slice of garlic into each incision, pushing it down into the flesh; lay the rosemary sprigs over the top of the chicken.

2   Arrange the potatoes around the sides of the chicken and season both the chicken and
potatoes lightly with salt and pepper. Pour the stock and wine into the dish and cover
with the lid.

3   Roast in the hot oven 1 hour. Remove the lid and leave to one side. Roast 40 minutes
longer until the juices from the chicken run clear when the thickest part of the thigh
is pierced with a skewer; if the juices look at all pink, cook for a little longer. Take the
chicken and potatoes out of the oven, replace the lid, and leave to stand in a warm
place 10 to 15 minutes.

4   Meanwhile, pour the cooking juices into a bowl and, using a spoon, skim off and discard
the layer of fat that rises to the top. Pour the juices into a saucepan and cook over high
heat 2 to 3 minutes to reduce. Serve with the chicken and potatoes, along with Roasted
Vegetables (see page 145), Italian-style Vegetables (see page 148), or Red Cabbage and
Apple (see page 147).

confit of duck

PREPARATION TIME **15 MINUTES, PLUS 2 DAYS CHILLING TIME**
COOKING TIME **2 HOURS**   SERVES **4**

4 large duck legs

2 tablespoons sea salt

2 garlic cloves, chopped

6 thyme sprigs

2¼ pounds goose or duck fat (about 4½ cups)

1   Arrange the duck legs, skin-side up, in a baking dish just large enough to hold them. Sprinkle the salt and garlic over and place the sprigs of thyme on top; cover with a lid and leave in the refrigerator 24 hours. Do not leave any longer, as the duck will become too salty.

2   Take the duck out of the dish and wipe thoroughly with paper towels to remove all the salt. Clean the dish and arrange the duck legs in it as before. Preheat the oven to 275°F.

3   Melt the goose or duck fat in a saucepan over low heat until starting to bubble, then pour it into the dish, covering all the duck pieces. Cover the dish and cook in the warm oven 1½ hours; take the duck out of the oven and leave to cool.

4   Take the cool duck legs out of the dish and put on a plate. Pour the remaining fat through a strainer into a bowl and discard any meat juices that are left on the bottom of the dish. Clean the dish and return the duck legs to it. Pour the strained fat over, cover the dish, and leave to chill in the refrigerator 24 hours.

5   Preheat the oven to 350°F. Remove the duck from the dish and wipe off most of the fat. Place the duck on a rack above a roasting pan and cook in the hot oven 20 minutes until the skin is crisp and golden and the meat is cooked through. Take the duck out of the oven and serve with Red Cabbage and Apple (see page 147) and Potatoes with Porcini Mushrooms (see page 142).

duck with cherry and juniper sauce

PREPARATION TIME **10 MINUTES**   COOKING TIME **25 TO 35 MINUTES**   SERVES **4**

3 cups halved and pitted cherries

5 juniper berries, crushed

³/₄ cup organic red wine

4 duck breast halves

¹/₂ teaspoon sea salt

1 tablespoon olive oil

1 teaspoon cornstarch

2 to 3 teaspoons sugar-free cherry jam

1   Preheat the oven to 350°F. Place the cherries and juniper berries in a heavy-bottom saucepan with the red wine. Bring to a boil over medium heat, then turn the heat down, cover with a lid, and leave to simmer 10 to 15 minutes until the cherries are soft, crushing them from time to time with the back of a wooden spoon.

2   Meanwhile, slash the skin of each duck piece and sprinkle a little salt over them. Heat the oil in a heavy-bottom skillet. Add the duck, skin-sides down, and cook over medium-high heat 4 to 5 minutes until the skins brown. Using a slotted spoon, lift the duck pieces from the pan and arrange in a roasting pan, skin-sides up; pour the juices from the pan over the top. Cook the duck in the hot oven 20 to 25 minutes until the skin is crisp, but the meat is still slightly pink in the middle.

3   When the cherries are soft, remove the pan from the heat and pour the mixture through a nonmetallic strainer set over a bowl, using the back of a metal spoon to push as much of the liquid through as possible. Discard the contents of the strainer. Rinse the saucepan, pour the liquid back into it, and return it to the heat. Bring to a boil, then turn the heat down and leave to simmer 15 to 20 minutes, stirring occasionally, until reduced by half.

4   Mix 1 teaspoon water with the cornstarch in a small bowl to make a smooth paste. Stir into the simmering cherry and juniper liquid and continue to simmer 4 to 5 minutes longer, stirring occasionally, until the sauce thickens; stir in the jam to taste.

5   When the duck has cooked, take it out of the oven and serve with the sauce, Olive Oil Herb Mash (see page 141) and vegetables.

dinners

pork with chestnuts, apple, and sage

PREPARATION TIME **10 MINUTES**   COOKING TIME **12 TO 15 MINUTES**   SERVES **4**

2 tablespoons olive oil

1 red onion, sliced lengthwise into 16 pieces

1 garlic clove, crushed

1¹⁄₂ pounds pork tenderloin, trimmed of fat and cut into
    bite-size chunks

4 ounces cooked, peeled chestnuts (fresh or
    vacuum-packed), cut into thirds

2 eating apples, peeled, quartered, and cored,
    and sliced lengthwise into 16 pieces

1 heaped tablespoon chopped sage leaves

sea salt and freshly ground black pepper

1 Heat the oil in a large, heavy-bottom saucepan. Add the onion and fry over gentle heat
2 minutes until just starting to turn golden. Stir in the garlic and then the pork, cover with a
lid, and cook 5 minutes, shaking the pan occasionally to turn the pork.

2 Remove the lid, add the chestnuts, apples, and sage, and cook 5 to 8 minutes until the
apple is soft and the liquid evaporates; season lightly with salt and pepper. Serve the
pork with Herb Mash made with a small handful sage instead of the parsley or cilantro
(see page 141), and vegetables.

pork

pork with umeboshi sauce

PREPARATION TIME **5 MINUTES**   COOKING TIME **11 TO 13 MINUTES**   SERVES **4**

4 tablespoons olive oil

1¹/₂ pounds pork tenderloin, trimmed of fat and
    cut into ³/₄-inch slices

2 bunches scallions, finely sliced

Umeboshi sauce:

scant ²/₃ cup honey

2 tablespoons umeboshi paste

2 tablespoons tamari soy sauce

1 teaspoon Chinese five-spice powder

1   Mix together the sauce ingredients in a measuring cup or a bowl until well blended.

2   Heat the oil in a large wok, add the pork, and stir-fry over high heat 5 to 6 minutes, stirring continuously. Add the scallions and stir-fry 1 minute.

3   Pour the umeboshi sauce over and cook 5 to 6 minutes, stirring occasionally, until the pork is cooked through and the sauce reduces a little. Serve with steamed rice.

gnocchi with mushroom and pancetta sauce

PREPARATION TIME **20 MINUTES**   COOKING TIME **25 TO 30 MINUTES**
ADDITIONAL TIME **MAKING THE SAUCE**   SERVES **4**

2 tablespoons olive oil

1 onion, finely chopped

2 garlic cloves, chopped

12 ounces nitrate-free pancetta, chopped

3½ cups sliced mushrooms

1 recipe quantity White Wine Sauce (see page 19)

sea salt and freshly ground black pepper

Gnocchi:

1½ pounds potatoes, peeled and cut into
    large chunks

3 egg yolks, beaten

¾ cup rice flour, plus extra for dusting

sea salt and freshly ground black pepper

1 To make the gnocchi, put the potatoes in a saucepan and cover with cold water. Place over high heat, bring to a boil, then turn the heat down, cover with a lid, and leave to simmer 15 to 20 minutes until tender. Meanwhile, heat the oil for the sauce in a heavy-bottom skillet. Add the onion and cook over medium heat 2 to 3 minutes until starting to turn golden. Stir in the garlic, then add the pancetta and fry 3 to 4 minutes. Add the mushrooms and cook 10 minutes, stirring occasionally.

2 When the potatoes are cooked, drain and mash well, then warm over low heat a few minutes. Tip into a large bowl and season lightly with salt and pepper, then beat in the egg yolks and flour, a little at a time, with a wooden spoon to form a smooth, slightly sticky dough.

3 Turn out the dough onto a surface dusted with rice flour and, with floured hands, knead and work it into a ball. Roll out to form into a long sausage about ¾ inch thick. Cut into ¾-inch pieces, then use the back of a fork to make grooves across the top of each piece; leave on the floured surface, making sure they do not overlap.

4 Fill a large pan with boiling water and set over medium heat so the water simmers gently. Add one-third of the prepared gnocchi and cook until they rise to the surface. Continue cooking 1 to 2 minutes longer, then remove with a slotted spoon and keep warm. Repeat with the remaining gnocchi.

5 Meanwhile, heat the white wine sauce over gentle heat until almost boiling. Stir in the pancetta mixture and season lightly with salt and pepper. Pour the hot sauce over the gnocchi and serve.

roasted squash, leek, and bacon risotto

PREPARATION TIME **5 MINUTES**   COOKING TIME **45 MINUTES**
ADDITIONAL TIME **MAKING THE STOCK**   SERVES **4**

2$^1/_4$ pounds butternut or other squash, peeled,
   seeded, and cut into bite-size pieces
3 tablespoons olive oil
1 quart Chicken or Vegetable Stock (see pages 24–5),
   or vegetable stock made from gluten-, yeast-, and
   dairy-free bouillon powder

1 small onion, finely chopped
2 garlic cloves, chopped
3 leeks, trimmed and sliced
7 ounces Canadian bacon, diced
scant 1$^1/_4$ cups arborio or other risotto rice
sea salt and freshly ground black pepper

1   Preheat the oven to 350°F. Place the squash in a roasting pan, drizzle 2 tablespoons of the oil over, and roast in the hot oven 45 minutes until tender.

2   When the squash has been roasting about 15 minutes, heat the stock in a saucepan until almost boiling, then turn the heat down, cover with a lid, and leave to simmer.

3   Heat the remaining oil in a large, heavy-bottom saucepan over medium heat. Add the onion and cook 2 to 3 minutes until just starting to turn golden. Stir in the garlic and cook about 30 seconds, then add the leeks and bacon. Lower the heat and continue cooking 3 to 4 minutes longer until the bacon cooks through and the leeks are soft.

4   Stir in the rice until it is well coated in oil, then add a ladle of the hot stock and stir until all the liquid is absorbed. Continue adding and stirring in the hot stock 18 to 20 minutes until the rice is soft, but still has a slight bite and all the liquid is absorbed.

5   Take the squash out of the oven and stir it carefully into the risotto. Season lightly with salt and pepper and serve with mixed salad greens.

dinners

lamb tagine

PREPARATION TIME **10 MINUTES**   COOKING TIME **1¾ HOURS**
ADDITIONAL TIME **MAKING THE STOCK AND THE RAS EL HANOUT**   SERVES **4**

lamb

¹/₂ cup Vegetable Stock (see page 25), or stock made
from gluten-, yeast-, and dairy-free bouillon powder

¹/₄ teaspoon saffron strands

3 tablespoons olive oil

1¹/₂ pounds boneless shoulder of lamb, trimmed of fat
and cut into bite-size pieces

2 onions, finely chopped

2 garlic cloves, crushed

2 tablespoons Ras el Hanout (see page 20)

heaped 1¹/₂ cups sugar-free dried unsulfured apricots
cut in half

²/₃ cup whole blanched almonds

3 tablespoons honey

1   Heat the stock in a saucepan until almost boiling; remove from the heat and stir in the saffron.

2   Heat 2 tablespoons of the oil in a large, heavy-bottom saucepan over medium heat. Add
the lamb and cook 3 to 4 minutes, stirring occasionally, until light brown. Remove the lamb
from the pan using a slotted spoon and put in a bowl; drain any juices into the bowl.

3   Heat the remaining oil in the pan over medium heat. Add the onions and cook 1 to 2 minutes
until slightly softened. Stir in the garlic, then the ras el hanout and cook about 30 seconds.
Return the lamb and juices to the pan and add the apricots, almonds, honey, and stock.

4   Bring to a boil, then turn the heat down, cover with a lid, and leave to simmer 1¹/₂ hours,
stirring occasionally. Skim any fat from the surface and serve with steamed rice
and vegetables.

lamb skewers with pomegranate and yogurt sauce

PREPARATION TIME **10 MINUTES, PLUS 30 MINUTES MARINATING TIME**
COOKING TIME **8 TO 12 MINUTES**   SERVES **4**

1 pound 2 ounces lamb tenderloin, trimmed of fat and
   cut into bite-size pieces

3 bell peppers (a mixture of red, orange, and yellow,
   or all one color), seeded and cut into large chunks

8 shallots, peeled and cut in half lengthwise

7 ounces button mushrooms

7 ounces cherry tomatoes

$^2/_3$ cup olive oil

Sauce:

1 pomegranate

1$^1/_4$ cups soy yogurt

1$^1/_2$ tablespoons finely chopped mint leaves

sea salt

1   Put the lamb in a large, flat, nonmetallic dish and season lightly with salt. Add the bell
peppers, shallots, mushrooms, and tomatoes and pour the oil over. Cover and leave to
marinate at least 30 minutes, while soaking 8 wooden skewers in water.

2   Preheat the broiler to high. Thread the lamb and vegetables onto the skewers, alternating
each ingredient. Place on the broiler rack and broil 4 to 6 minutes on each side until the
lamb is crisp and brown on the outside, but still pink in the middle.

3   Meanwhile, to make the sauce, halve the pomegranate and, holding each half over a large
bowl, bash the outer skin with a wooden spoon until all the seeds fall out into the bowl.
You'll need to bash the skin a few times before the seeds begin to fall out, but they will.
Stir in the yogurt and mint and season lightly with salt. Serve the skewers with the sauce
and steamed rice.

beef stroganoff

PREPARATION TIME **5 MINUTES**　　COOKING TIME **12 TO 20 MINUTES**　　SERVES **4**

2 tablespoons dairy-free margarine

2 small red onions, finely chopped

1 to 1½ teaspoons paprika

4 cups sliced button mushrooms

1¼ pounds beef tenderloin, cut into strips

3 tablespoons olive oil

1⅔ cups soy yogurt

1 large handful flat-leaf parsley, finely chopped

sea salt and freshly ground black pepper

1　Melt the margarine in a large, heavy-bottom saucepan. Add the onions and 1 teaspoon paprika and cook over medium heat 2 to 3 minutes until starting to turn golden. Stir in the mushrooms and cook 5 to 7 minutes; tip the onions and mushrooms onto a plate.

2　Season the steak lightly with salt and pepper. Heat 2 tablespoons of the oil in the pan over high heat. Add half the seasoned steak and cook 2 to 4 minutes, turning, until brown. Remove from the pan using a slotted spoon and leave to one side. Repeat with the remaining oil and steak.

3　Return the onions and mushrooms to the pan. Using a whisk or an electric mixer, blend the yogurt until smooth. Stir the yogurt into the mixture and heat through gently 1 to 2 minutes, taking care not to overcook, as the yogurt will curdle. Stir in the steak and parsley, then check the seasoning and add more paprika, if required. Serve with steamed rice and vegetables.

spaghetti with meatballs

PREPARATION TIME **10 MINUTES**   COOKING TIME **20 TO 25 MINUTES**
ADDITIONAL TIME **MAKING THE SAUCE**   SERVES **4**

3 tablespoons olive oil

1 onion, finely chopped

1 garlic clove, chopped

1 pound 6 ounces ground steak

1 egg, beaten

1 large handful flat-leaf parsley, finely chopped

14 ounces gluten-free spaghetti, or other gluten-free
    pasta shape

1 recipe quantity Tomato and Bell Pepper Sauce
    (see page 18)

sea salt and freshly ground black pepper

beef

1   Heat 1 tablespoon of the oil in a large, heavy-bottom skillet. Add the onion and cook over medium heat 2 to 3 minutes until turning golden. Add the garlic and cook 30 seconds.

2   Tip the onion and garlic into a large mixing bowl. Add the ground steak, egg, and parsley and season lightly with salt and pepper. Mix well to combine the ingredients, then divide the mixture into 16 portions and shape each into a ball with your hands.

3   Heat the tomato and bell pepper sauce in a large, heavy-bottom saucepan over a gentle heat until almost boiling and let simmer.

4   Heat another tablespoon of the oil in the skillet. Add half the meatballs and cook over medium heat 8 to 10 minutes, moving them around the pan so they brown and cook through evenly. Remove from the skillet with a slotted spoon and add to the saucepan with the tomato and bell pepper sauce. Repeat with the remaining meatballs.

5   Meanwhile, bring a large saucepan of water to a boil. Add the remaining oil, then the spaghetti, pushing it down into the water as it softens. Cook over medium heat 8 to 10 minutes, or according to the package directions, stirring frequently to make sure it does not stick together; drain, then rinse well with boiling water, and drain again. Serve with the meatballs in the tomato and bell pepper sauce and with mixed salad greens.

steak with roasted asparagus and hollandaise sauce

PREPARATION TIME **5 MINUTES**   COOKING TIME **10 TO 12 MINUTES**
ADDITIONAL TIME **MAKING THE SAUCE**   SERVES **4**

1 pound 2 ounces asparagus, woody ends removed

2¹/₂ tablespoons olive oil

4 filet mignons

1 recipe quantity Hollandaise Sauce (see page 19)

sea salt and freshly ground black pepper

1   Preheat the oven to 350°F. Place the asparagus on a baking tray. Drizzle 1¹/₂ tablespoons of the oil over and roast in the hot oven 10 to 12 minutes until cooked through and tender.

2   Meanwhile, heat the remaining oil in a large, heavy-bottom skillet. Season the steaks lightly with salt and pepper, add to the pan, and cook over medium heat 3 to 5 minutes on each side for medium-rare or another 1 to 2 minutes for well done. Alternatively, brush the steaks with the remaining oil and cook under a hot broiler.

3   Take the asparagus out of the oven and serve with the steak and the hot hollandaise sauce, and with boiled new potatoes or baked potatoes.

ginger chili tuna

PREPARATION TIME **10 MINUTES, PLUS 1 HOUR MARINATING TIME**
COOKING TIME **6 TO 8 MINUTES**   SERVES **4**

4 tuna steaks

1 tablespoon olive oil

Marinade:
³/₄-inch piece fresh gingerroot, peeled and
    finely chopped
2 large garlic cloves, finely chopped
1 small or ¹/₂ large fresh red chili, seeded and
    finely chopped

2 heaped tablespoons chopped mint leaves

2 heaped tablespoons chopped basil leaves

1 handful cilantro leaves, finely chopped

3 tablespoons olive oil

1 tablespoon Thai fish sauce

juice of 2 limes

1   Place the tuna in a shallow, nonmetallic dish. Mix together all the marinade ingredients in a
     bowl or measuring jug and pour over the tuna. Cover with a lid or plastic wrap and leave to
     marinate in the refrigerator at least one hour, preferably longer.

2   Heat the oil in a heavy-bottom skillet over medium heat. Place the tuna in the hot pan,
     spoon the marinade on top of each steak, and pour the remaining liquid into the pan. Cook
     3 to 4 minutes on each side until the tuna is light brown on the outside but remains slightly
     pink in the middle. Serve with Vegetable Stir-fry (see page 146).

salmon with honey and ginger

PREPARATION TIME **5 MINUTES, PLUS 1 HOUR MARINATING TIME**
COOKING TIME **30 TO 35 MINUTES**   SERVES **4**

4 salmon fillets

1-inch piece fresh gingerroot, peeled and
finely chopped

1 bunch scallions, finely chopped

2 tablespoons tamari soy sauce

2 tablespoons honey

1   Place the salmon fillets in a large baking dish, skin-side down. Sprinkle the ginger and scallions over the top, then pour the tamari soy sauce and honey over; cover with a lid and leave to marinate in the refrigerator at least one hour, preferably longer.

2   Preheat the oven to 350°F. Place the dish in the hot oven and cook 30 to 35 minutes until the salmon is cooked through.

3   Take the salmon fillets out of the oven and serve with the sauce from the dish and steamed rice or Herb Mash (see page 141) and vegetables.

salmon fishcakes

PREPARATION TIME **15 MINUTES, PLUS 30 MINUTES CHILLING TIME**
COOKING TIME **35 TO 45 MINUTES**   SERVES **4**

1 pound 2 ounces salmon fillets

2 tablespoons olive oil

1 pound 2 ounces potatoes, peeled and
    cut into large chunks

2 extra-large eggs, beaten

gram flour for dusting

polenta or cornmeal for dusting

sea salt and freshly ground black pepper

1 Preheat the oven to 350°F. Place the salmon in a baking dish and drizzle half of the oil over. Cover and bake in the hot oven 20 to 25 minutes until cooked through.

2 Meanwhile, put the potatoes in a saucepan and cover with cold water. Place over high heat, bring to a boil, then turn the heat down, cover with a lid, and leave to simmer 15 to 20 minutes until tender. Drain, return to the saucepan, and heat gently 1 to 2 minutes to dry out. Mash coarsely.

3 Take the salmon out of the oven, remove and discard the skin and any brown meat, and flake with a fork, reserving any juices. Mix together the flaked salmon, mashed potatoes, half the beaten eggs, the reserved cooking juices, and some salt and pepper, taking care not to break up the fish too much. With wet hands, shape the salmon mixture into 8 balls, then flatten them slightly to form fishcakes.

4 Spread the gram flour out on a plate and the polenta or cornmeal out on a second plate. Dip each fishcake into the gram flour to coat it, then into the remaining beaten egg, then finally into the polenta or cornmeal until well coated. Place on a clean plate, cover with plastic wrap, and leave to chill in the refrigerator at least 30 minutes.

5 Heat the remaining oil in a large, heavy-bottom skillet over medium heat. Add half the fishcakes and cook 4 to 5 minutes on each side until golden brown. Keep warm while you cook the remaining fishcakes. Serve with vegetables or mixed salad leaves.

fish & shellfish

dinners

herbed monkfish wrapped in prosciutto

PREPARATION TIME **10 MINUTES, PLUS 2 HOURS CHILLING TIME**
COOKING TIME **12 TO 16 MINUTES**   SERVES **4**

1¹/₄ pounds monkfish fillet, cut lengthwise into
    four long pieces
1 large handful chopped cilantro leaves
1 large handful chopped flat-leaf parsley

juice of 1 lemon
6 tablespoons olive oil
8 slices nitrate-free prosciutto
sea salt and freshly ground black pepper

1 Place the monkfish pieces in a shallow, nonmetallic dish. Mix together the cilantro, parsley, lemon juice, and oil in a bowl and season lightly with salt and pepper. Pour over the fish, cover the dish, and leave to marinate in the refrigerator at least 2 hours.

2 Preheat the broiler to high. Place 2 slices of prosciutto, side by side, on a clean surface. Remove one piece of monkfish from the dish, making sure it is well coated in chopped herbs from the marinade, and lay it across the slices of ham. Carefully roll the ham around the herbed fish; repeat with the remaining pieces of fish and ham.

3 Arrange the ham-wrapped pieces of fish on the broiler rack and cook under the hot broiler 6 to 8 minutes on each side until the fish is cooked. Serve with boiled new potatoes and Italian-style Vegetables (see page 148).

baked sea bass with tarragon sauce and fennel puree

PREPARATION TIME **15 MINUTES**   COOKING TIME **1 HOUR**   ADDITIONAL TIME **MAKING THE STOCKS**   SERVES **4**

3 tablespoons olive oil

3 shallots, finely chopped

1¹/₂ cups organic dry white wine

2 cups Fish Stock (see page 25), or vegetable stock
made from gluten-, yeast-, and dairy-free
bouillon powder

12 tarragon sprigs

2 large or 4 medium sea bass, gutted and cleaned

1 tablespoon cornstarch

²/₃ cup sugar-free soymilk

1¹/₄ ounces silken tofu

Fennel puree:

2 fennel bulbs, trimmed and sliced lengthwise

³/₄ cup Vegetable Stock (see page 25), or stock
made as before

sea salt and freshly ground black pepper

1   Preheat the oven to 350°F. Heat 2 tablespoons of the oil in a large, heavy-bottom saucepan over medium heat. Add the shallots and cook 1 to 2 minutes until starting to turn golden. Add the wine and bring to a boil, then turn the heat down and leave to simmer 15 to 20 minutes until the liquid reduces. Add the fish stock and return to a boil, then turn the heat down and leave to simmer 20 minutes longer.

2   Meanwhile, place the fennel and vegetable stock in a saucepan and bring to a boil. Lower the heat, cover with a lid, and simmer 10 minutes until the fennel is soft. Using an electric mixer, blend to form a smooth puree. Alternatively, blend in a blender or food processor; season lightly with salt and pepper and keep warm.

3   Divide 8 of the tarragon sprigs between the fish cavities. Place the fish in a baking dish, drizzle the remaining oil over, and bake in the hot oven 20 to 30 minutes until cooked.

4   Mix 1 tablespoon water and the cornstarch in a bowl to form a smooth paste. Add the milk and tofu and, using an electric mixer, blend the mixture until smooth. Pour into the stock mixture, turn the heat up, and bring the sauce to a boil, stirring constantly. Turn the heat down and leave to simmer 8 to 10 minutes until the sauce is thick enough to coat the back of a spoon. Chop the remaining tarragon finely and stir into the sauce.

5   Take the fish out of the oven and serve with the fennel puree, the tarragon sauce, and boiled new potatoes.

fish & shellfish

salmon and shrimp fish pie

PREPARATION TIME **10 MINUTES**   COOKING TIME **50 TO 60 MINUTES**
ADDITIONAL TIME **MAKING THE STOCK AND THE SAUCE**   SERVES **4**

1 pound 2 ounces salmon fillets

1 bay leaf

scant 3 cups Fish Stock (see page 25), or vegetable
    stock made from gluten-, yeast-, and dairy-free
    bouillon powder

2¼ pounds potatoes, peeled and cut into large chunks

4 tablespoons sugar-free soymilk

1 egg, beaten

4 tablespoons dairy-free margarine

9 ounces cooked, shelled jumbo shrimp, deveined

1 recipe quantity Béchamel Sauce (see page 18)

sea salt and freshly ground black pepper

1 Place the salmon in a large saucepan. Add the bay leaf and fish stock and bring to a boil over medium heat. Turn the heat down, cover with a lid, and leave to simmer 8 minutes until the fish is cooked through. Remove the salmon from the pan, using a slotted spoon, and leave to cool; reserve the cooking liquid.

2 Meanwhile, preheat the oven to 400°F. Put the potatoes in a large saucepan and cover with cold water. Place over a high heat, bring to a boil, then turn the heat down, cover with a lid, and leave to simmer 15 to 20 minutes until tender. Drain, stir in 4 tablespoons of the reserved fish cooking liquid, the soymilk, egg, and margarine, and season lightly with salt and pepper. Mash until well blended and smooth, using an electric mixer if you want a very smooth result.

3 When the salmon has cooled enough to handle, remove and discard the skin and any brown meat. Break into large, bite-size chunks and arrange in the bottom of a 10-cup baking dish. Place the shrimp on top and pour the béchamel sauce over to cover the fish.

4 Spoon the mashed potato over, spreading it evenly. Bake in the hot oven 35 to 40 minutes until the top is golden, then take it out of the oven and serve with vegetables.

moules marinière

PREPARATION TIME **15 MINUTES**   COOKING TIME **5 TO 7 MINUTES**   SERVES **4**

4¹/₂ pounds fresh mussels in their shells

4 tablespoons dairy-free margarine

2 small onions, finely chopped

1 garlic clove, finely chopped

1 cup organic dry white wine

4 tablespoons soy yogurt

1 large handful chopped flat-leaf parsley

sea salt and freshly ground black pepper

1 Scrub the mussels thoroughly with a stiff brush under cold running water to remove all traces of grit, then remove any barnacles or other debris attached to the shells and pull off and discard the "beard" of fibrous material around the edge; rinse again and discard any mussels that are open.

2 Melt the margarine in a large, heavy-bottom saucepan over medium heat. Add the onions and cook 2 to 3 minutes until they start to turn golden. Stir in the garlic and cook 30 seconds.

3 Add the mussels and wine, turn up the heat a little, cover with a lid, and cook 3 to 4 minutes until the mussels open; discard any that do not open.

4 Using a whisk or an electric mixer, blend the yogurt until smooth. Stir the yogurt and chopped parsley into the wine and season lightly with salt and pepper. Heat through briefly and serve with fries or chunks of bread (see pages 23–4) and a green salad.

broiled shrimp with mango salsa

PREPARATION TIME **15 MINUTES, PLUS 1 HOUR MARINATING TIME**
COOKING TIME **8 TO 11 MINUTES** SERVES **4**

1½ pounds raw, shelled jumbo shrimp,
    tails attached, deveined

6 scallions, finely sliced

³/₄-inch piece fresh gingerroot, peeled and
    finely chopped

2 garlic cloves, finely chopped

½ large fresh red chili, seeded and very
    finely chopped

1 large handful chopped cilantro leaves

juice of 2 limes

4 tablespoons olive oil

10 ounces rice noodles

Mango salsa:

2 large ripe mangoes

6 scallions, finely sliced

1 large fresh red chili, seeded and
    very finely chopped

1 large handful chopped cilantro leaves

juice of 2 limes

1   Place the shrimp in a shallow, nonmetallic dish and sprinkle the scallions, ginger, garlic, chili, cilantro, lime juice, and oil over. Mix to combine, cover the bowl with a lid or plastic wrap, and leave in the refrigerator to marinate at least 1 hour, preferably longer.

2   Meanwhile, prepare the salsa. With a sharp knife, carefully slice the mango down the sides, avoiding the pit. Cut the flesh inside the slices into small squares, cutting down to the peel but not piercing it, and scoop out with a spoon. Peel the remains of the mango, slice the flesh from the pit, and place all the flesh in a mixing bowl. Add the scallions, chili, cilantro, and lime juice and stir to mix well.

3   When the shrimp have marinated, preheat the broiler to high. Remove the shrimp from the marinade and arrange on a rack over a broiler pan. Pour the marinade mixture through a sieve into a large saucepan and discard the pulp. Stir in the rice noodles and pour over enough boiling water to cover. Place over medium heat and cook 4 to 5 minutes until the noodles are soft; drain and keep warm.

4   Cook the shrimp under the hot broiler 2 to 3 minutes on each side until pink and firm. Serve with the noodles and mango salsa.

fish & shellfish

rice wrapper rolls with mint and shrimp

PREPARATION TIME **45 MINUTES**   SERVES **4**

3 ounces rice vermicelli

16 round rice wrappers

1 bunch mint, leaves only

64 cooked, shelled small shrimp, deveined,
   about 14 ounces total weight

2 carrots, peeled and cut into matchsticks

$^1/_2$ cucumber, cut into matchsticks

4 scallions, white part only, sliced thinly lengthwise,
   then each part chopped into eight

tamari soy sauce, for dipping

1   Place the rice vermicelli in a large bowl, cover with boiling water, and leave to stand
5 to 6 minutes until the vermicelli is soft. Rinse well under cold running water, then drain.

2   Refill the large bowl with fresh boiling water and place one rice wrapper in it. Leave to
stand 30 seconds until the wrapper is soft. Fold a damp clean dish towel in half, carefully
remove the rice wrapper from the water and place it on top of the cloth.

3   Arrange 3 to 5 mint leaves, depending on size, horizontally on the wrapper, slightly off-
center toward you, leaving a gap on each side. Put 3 to 4 shrimp on top, followed by
3 to 4 sticks of carrot, then 3 to 4 sticks of cucumber. Add a few slices of scallion and
cover with a little of the vermicelli.

4   Fold the side of the rice wrapper nearest to you over the stack of vegetables and shrimp,
making sure it is tight, then fold in the ends. Carefully roll the stack until all the rice wrapper
is wrapped around it. Set aside on a plate, covered with a damp cloth, while you prepare
the others. Repeat with the remaining sheets of rice wrapper, mint, shrimp, and vegetables,
refreshing the boiling water whenever necessary. Serve the rolls with tamari soy sauce
for dipping.

mushroom, spinach, and egg stack

PREPARATION TIME **10 TO 15 MINUTES**   COOKING TIME **10 TO 15 MINUTES**
ADDITIONAL TIME **MAKING THE POLENTA**   SERVES **4**

4 tablespoons olive oil

4 large, open mushrooms, about 14 ounces total
    weight, stalks removed

3 large garlic cloves, finely chopped

14 ounces button mushrooms cut into quarters

14 ounces baby leaf spinach

1¼ cups soy yogurt

4 extra-large eggs

1 recipe quantity freshly cooked Quick Polenta,
    broiled or fried (see page 143)

sea salt and freshly ground black pepper

1   Heat 1 tablespoon of the oil in a large, heavy-bottom saucepan over medium heat. Add the
mushrooms, open-side up, and cook 3 to 4 minutes until cooked through. Remove them
from the pan and keep warm.

2   Wipe the pan clean and heat the remaining oil in it over medium heat. Add the garlic and
cook about 30 seconds. Add the button mushrooms and cook 4 to 5 minutes, stirring
continuously, then the spinach and cook 2 to 3 minutes, stirring, until it wilts and some of
the liquid evaporates. Using a whisk or an electric mixer, blend the yogurt until smooth.
Remove the pan from the heat, pour in the yogurt, and stir gently. Season lightly with salt
and pepper, then cover to keep the mixture warm.

3   Meanwhile, bring a large saucepan of water to a boil, then lower the heat to a simmer. Stir
the water vigorously, crack the eggs one at a time into a cup, and, making sure the water is
still swirling around, gently slip them into the water. Poach 3 to 4 minutes until the whites are
set, but still soft, and the yolks are still runny.

4   Place one slice of broiled or fried polenta on each plate and put one large mushroom on
top. Spoon a little of the warm spinach and mushroom mixture on top of the large mushrooms
and place the rest around the sides, on the polenta. Remove the eggs from the pan with a
slotted spoon, place one on top of each stack and serve.

chickpea and tomato stew

PREPARATION TIME **10 MINUTES, PLUS OVERNIGHT SOAKING TIME**
COOKING TIME **1½ TO 2 HOURS**   SERVES **4**

scant 1½ cups dried chickpeas, or 1½ cans (14-ounce)
    salt-free chickpeas, drained and rinsed

2¼ pounds vine-ripened tomatoes

2 tablespoons olive oil

1 onion, finely chopped

2 large garlic cloves, chopped

½ teaspoon sweet smoked paprika

¼ teaspoon paprika

½ teaspoon dried chili flakes

1 cup soy yogurt

10 ounces baby leaf spinach

sea salt and freshly ground black pepper

1   If using dried chickpeas, place them in a bowl, cover with cold water, and leave to soak overnight or at least 12 hours.

2   The next day, drain the chickpeas, then rinse thoroughly. Put the peas in a large saucepan, cover with fresh water, and bring to a boil. Boil rapidly 10 minutes, then turn the heat down, cover with a lid, and leave to simmer 1 to 1½ hours until tender. Drain thoroughly.

3   With a sharp knife, cut a cross in the skin of each tomato, then place them in a large, heat-proof bowl, and pour enough boiling water over to cover; leave to stand 2 to 3 minutes, then drain. Peel off and discard the skins, then chop each tomato into about 8 pieces.

4   Heat the oil in a large, heavy-bottom saucepan over gentle heat. Add the onion and cook 2 to 3 minutes until golden in color. Stir in the garlic, then the sweet smoked paprika, paprika, and chili flakes, and cook 1 to 2 minutes, stirring continuously. Add the tomatoes, turn the heat up slightly, and cook 5 minutes, using the back of a wooden spoon to press down on the tomato pieces. Finally, add the cooked or canned chickpeas and cook 10 to 12 minutes until the sauce reduces by about half.

5   Using a whisk or an electric mixer, blend the yogurt until smooth. Stir into the tomato mixture, turn the heat down, and leave to simmer 10 minutes longer until the chickpeas are tender, stirring occasionally. Season lightly with salt and pepper, then stir in the spinach and cook about 1 minute until the spinach wilts and is well mixed in. Serve with steamed rice.

vegetarian

pasta puttanesca

PREPARATION TIME **10 MINUTES**   COOKING TIME **20 TO 25 MINUTES**   SERVES **4**

2¼ pounds vine-ripened tomatoes

3 tablespoons olive oil

4 garlic cloves, finely chopped

20 anchovies in oil, drained and chopped
    (optional)

4 tablespoons capers in brine, rinsed

2 large fresh red chilies, seeded and finely chopped

2 handfuls chopped parsley

14 ounces gluten-free penne, or other gluten-free
    pasta shape

sea salt and freshly ground black pepper

1   Cut a cross in the skin of each tomato and place in a large heatproof bowl. Pour boiling water over to cover and leave to stand 2 to 3 minutes. Take the tomatoes out of the water and peel off and discard the skins. Chop each tomato into eight pieces.

2   Heat 2 tablespoons of the oil in a heavy-bottom saucepan. Add the garlic, and anchovies if using, and cook over low heat 1 minute. Add the tomatoes, bring to a boil, then turn the heat down and simmer 15 to 20 minutes until the sauce has reduced and thickened.

3   Stir the capers and chilies into the tomato sauce and cook over low heat 4 to 5 minutes. Stir the chopped parsley through the sauce, season lightly with salt and pepper, and cook one minute.

4   Meanwhile, bring a large saucepan of water to a boil. Add the remaining oil, then the pasta. Cook over medium heat 8 to 10 minutes, or according to the package directions, stirring frequently so the pasta does not stick together. Drain and rinse well with boiling water, then drain again. Serve with the sauce and mixed salad leaves.

pasta primavera

PREPARATION TIME **15 MINUTES**   COOKING TIME **11 TO 14 MINUTES**
ADDITIONAL TIME **MAKING THE STOCK**   SERVES **4**

1½ pounds peas in their pods, shelled
   (1½ cups shelled)
14 ounces asparagus, woody ends removed,
   cut into thirds
7 ounces thin green beans, trimmed and cut in half
2 tablespoons olive oil
14 ounces gluten-free pasta
scant 2 cups soy yogurt
5 tablespoons organic dry white wine

5 tablespoons Vegetable Stock (see page 25),
   or stock made from gluten-, yeast-, and
   dairy-free bouillon powder
1 onion, finely chopped
2 garlic cloves, chopped
2½ ounces arugula, coarsely chopped
1½ heaped tablespoons chopped mint leaves
1½ heaped tablespoons chopped flat-leaf parsley
sea salt and freshly ground black pepper

1   Place the peas, asparagus, and beans in a steamer and cook over medium heat
   3 to 4 minutes until just tender, but still slightly crunchy; drain.

2   Bring a large saucepan of water to a boil. Add 1 tablespoon of the oil, then the pasta.
   Cook over medium heat 8 to 10 minutes, or according to the package directions, stirring
   frequently so the pasta does not stick together.

3   Meanwhile, spoon the yogurt into a bowl, then, using a whisk or an electric mixer, blend
   until smooth. Add the wine and stock and blend again; season lightly with salt and pepper.

4   Heat the remaining oil in a large, heavy-bottom saucepan. Add the onion and cook over
   medium heat 2 to 3 minutes until starting to turn golden. Stir in the garlic, then pour in the
   yogurt mixture, lower the heat, and cook gently 1 minute. Stir in the cooked vegetables and
   then the arugula, mint, and parsley and cook 1 minute to heat through, taking care not to
   cook for too long, or the yogurt will curdle.

5   Drain the pasta and rinse well with boiling water, then drain again. Serve with the sauce
   and mixed salad greens.

roasted vegetable tarts

PREPARATION TIME **20 MINUTES**   COOKING TIME **65 TO 75 MINUTES**
ADDITIONAL TIME **MAKING THE PASTRY DOUGH**   MAKES **4**

3 bell peppers (a mixture of red, orange, and yellow or
    all one color), seeded and cut into quarters
3 tablespoons olive oil
3 large vine-ripened tomatoes, each cut into 8 pieces
1 onion, cut into 16 pieces
dairy-free margarine, for greasing

1 recipe quantity Rich Piecrust Dough,
    or gluten-free version (see page 21)
rice flour for dusting
2 extra-large eggs plus 6 extra-large egg yolks, beaten
4 tablespoons sugar-free soymilk
sea salt and freshly ground black pepper

1 Preheat the oven to 350°F. Arrange the bell peppers, cut-side down, and the tomatoes and onions on two baking trays and drizzle the oil over. Place both trays of vegetables in the hot oven and roast 20 to 25 minutes. Remove the tomatoes and onions, but leave the bell peppers to roast 10 minutes longer until the skins are black.

2 Put the bell peppers in a plastic bag and leave 2 to 3 minutes; remove from the bag and peel off the skins. Turn the oven up to 400°F. Grease four 5-inch tartlet pans, ³/₄ inch deep, with removable bottoms with dairy-free margarine.

3 Gently roll out the dough on a surface liberally dusted with rice flour until about ¹/₈ inch thick. Using a biscuit cutter that is slightly larger in diameter than the pans, to allow enough dough for the sides, cut out four dough circles, discarding any extra pastry; be very gentle, as the dough will still be slightly sticky.

4 Lift the dough circles into each pan (you may need to use a metal spatula) and press down lightly to remove any pockets of air. Line each tartlet shell with a piece of baking parchment and cover with baking beans. Place the tartlet pans on a baking tray and bake in the hot oven 8 to 10 minutes until firm and lightly golden. Take the tartlet shells out of the oven and remove the parchment and beans. Turn the oven down to 350°F.

5 Divide the roasted onion between the tartlet shells, then top each with 4 tomato pieces and 2 bell pepper quarters. Mix the eggs, egg yolks, and soymilk together in a bowl and season lightly with salt and pepper. Pour the mixture over the vegetables.

6 Bake the filled tartlet shells in the hot oven 25 to 30 minutes until the filling is cooked through. Take them out of the oven, leave to cool in the pans until the filling has set. Carefully ease them out onto a plate and serve with vegetables or mixed salad greens.

vegetarian

side dishes

Fill your plate with the delicious side dishes featured in these pages.

Creamy mashed potato with herbs or with olive oil is great with dishes

such as Salmon with Honey and Ginger, for example, while the depth of

the flavors in Potatoes with Porcini Mushrooms complements the Confit

of Duck beautifully. Then there's Quick Polenta, which you can make in

a matter of minutes and serve with strong tastes, such as Chicken with

Salsa Verde. Vegetables can make a meal spectacular—the combination of

Vegetable Stir-fry with the Ginger Chili Tuna, for example, adds variety and

zing to the meal, while the addition of Italian-style Vegetables to the Herbed

Monkfish Wrapped in Prosciutto brings out the complexity of tastes. So,

sign up for an organic delivery program and invest in a great peeler!

herb mash

PREPARATION TIME **5 MINUTES**   COOKING TIME **15 TO 20 MINUTES**   SERVES **4**

1³/₄ pounds potatoes, peeled and cut into
    large chunks
5 tablespoons dairy-free margarine, diced

scant ²/₃ cup sugar-free soymilk
1 bunch flat-leaf parsley or cilantro
sea salt and freshly ground black pepper

1 Put the potatoes in a saucepan and cover with cold water. Place over high heat, bring to a boil, then turn the heat down, cover with a lid, and leave to simmer 15 to 20 minutes until tender; drain, then mash thoroughly until smooth. For very smooth mash, use an electric mixer.

2 Stir in the margarine with the milk and chopped parsley or cilantro, then season lightly with salt and pepper and serve.

To make Olive Oil Herb Mash, follow the method above, substituting 3 tablespoons olive oil for the dairy-free margarine.

VARIATION

potatoes with porcini mushrooms

PREPARATION TIME **10 MINUTES PLUS 30 MINUTES SOAKING TIME**
COOKING TIME **1¼ TO 1½ HOURS**   SERVES **4**

4 ounces dried porcini mushrooms, or dried mixed
    wild mushrooms
dairy-free margarine for greasing

2 pounds potatoes, peeled and thinly sliced
4 tablespoons olive oil
sea salt and freshly ground black pepper

1   Place the mushrooms in a bowl, cover with boiling water, and leave to stand 30 minutes.

2   Preheat the oven to 350°F. Grease a large baking dish with a lid with dairy-free margarine. Drain the mushrooms, reserving ²/₃ cup of the liquid.

3   Cover the base of the prepared dish with a layer of potato slices. Top with a layer of mushrooms and season lightly with salt and pepper. Repeat the layers until all the mushrooms and potato slices are used up, finishing with a layer of potato. Pour the reserved liquid from the mushrooms over, then drizzle the olive oil over the top.

4   Cover with a lid and bake in the hot oven 45 minutes. Uncover and return to the oven 30 to 40 minutes longer until the potatoes are tender and the top layer is brown and crispy. Take it out of the oven and serve.

quick polenta

PREPARATION TIME **10 MINUTES**   COOKING TIME **5 TO 16 MINUTES**   SERVES **4**

heaped 1¹/₂ cups quick-cook polenta

¹/₂ teaspoon dried chili flakes (optional)

5 to 6 tablespoons olive oil

sea salt and freshly ground black pepper

1   Pour 1 quart water into a large, heavy-bottom saucepan and bring to a boil. Lower the heat and pour the polenta in slowly, stirring all the while, then add the dried chili flakes, if using. Cook gently 5 to 6 minutes, stirring occasionally, until thick. Stir in 5 tablespoons of the olive oil and remove from the heat.

2   Season lightly with salt and pepper and either serve or spoon the mixture into a baking tray, smoothing it into a flat layer, and leave to stand 5 to 10 minutes until set.

3   Cut the set polenta into four thick slices, then either cook under a hot broiler 2 to 3 minutes on each side until golden brown, or fry in 1 tablespoon olive oil in a large, heavy-bottom skillet over medium heat 4 to 5 minutes on each side until golden brown, and serve.

roasted vegetables

PREPARATION TIME **15 MINUTES**   COOKING TIME **1½ HOURS**   SERVES **4**

4 large sweet potatoes, peeled and cut into quarters

1 large butternut or other squash, peeled, seeded,
   and cut into same-size pieces as the sweet potatoes

12 large carrots, peeled and cut into thin sticks

6 tablespoons olive oil

2 garlic cloves, finely sliced

1 large fresh red chili, seeded and finely chopped
   (optional)

1   Preheat the oven to 350°F. Place all the vegetables in a large roasting pan. Drizzle the oil over them and toss well to coat, then sprinkle with the garlic, and the chili if using.

2   Roast in the hot oven 1½ hours, turning every half hour, until crisp and golden brown, then take the vegetables out of the oven and serve.

side dishes

vegetable stir-fry

PREPARATION TIME **10 MINUTES**   COOKING TIME **4 TO 6 MINUTES**   SERVES **4**

2 tablespoons olive oil

1 bunch scallions, finely sliced

³/₄-inch piece fresh gingerroot, peeled and
    finely chopped

¹/₂ large fresh red chili, seeded and finely chopped

1 lemongrass stalk, finely chopped

2 large garlic cloves, finely chopped

9 ounces thin green beans, cut into 2-inch pieces

7 ounces sugar-snap peas

10 ounces bok choy, sliced into thirds widthwise,
    stems and leaves separated

2 tablespoons tamari soy sauce

1 heaped tablespoon chopped mint leaves

1 heaped tablespoon chopped basil leaves

1 large handful chopped cilantro leaves

1   Heat a large wok over medium-high heat until hot. Add the oil and swirl it around the wok.
    Stir in the scallions, then the gingerroot, chili, lemongrass, and finally the garlic and stir-fry
    30 seconds. Add the beans and stir-fry one minute.

2   Add the sugar-snap peas and the pieces of bok choy stem. Pour in the tamari soy sauce
    and 4 tablespoons water. Stir thoroughly and cook 1 to 2 minutes. Add the bok choy leaves
    and cook 1 to 2 minutes until all the vegetables are cooked, but remain slightly crunchy.

3   Remove from the heat and stir in the chopped herbs and serve.

red cabbage and apple

PREPARATION TIME **10 MINUTES**   COOKING TIME **2½ HOURS**   SERVES **4**

4 teaspoons dairy-free margarine, plus extra
    for greasing

1 red cabbage, about 1¹/₂ pounds, halved lengthwise,
    core removed, and leaves diced

4 cups peeled, cored, and diced apples

1 onion, finely chopped

1 garlic clove, finely chopped

1 teaspoon ground allspice

3 tablespoons date syrup or honey

2 tablespoons white wine vinegar

sea salt and freshly ground black pepper

1   Preheat the oven to 300°F. Grease a large baking dish with dairy-free margarine.

2   Arrange about one third of the cabbage on the bottom of the prepared dish. Cover with
about one third of the apples and one third of the chopped onion. Sprinkle a pinch of the
chopped garlic, about one third of the allspice, and 1 tablespoon of the date syrup or
honey over, then season lightly with salt and pepper; repeat this layering twice.

3   Pour the vinegar over the ingredients and dot with pieces of the margarine. Cover with a lid
and bake in the hot oven 2¹/₂ hours, stirring every 30 minutes, until the cabbage is tender.
Take out of the oven and serve.

italian-style vegetables

PREPARATION TIME **10 MINUTES**   COOKING TIME **20 TO 25 MINUTES**
ADDITIONAL TIME **MAKING THE STOCK**   SERVES **4**

side dishes

2 fennel bulbs

3 tablespoons olive oil

3 garlic cloves, finely sliced

3 cups chopped Savoy cabbage leaves,
    tough stems removed

3 cups chopped chard leaves, tough stems removed

1 cup Chicken or Vegetable Stock (see pages 24–5),
    or vegetable stock made from gluten-, yeast-,
    and dairy-free bouillon powder

5 ounces nitrate-free pancetta, diced

10 ounces baby leaf spinach

1 large handful chopped flat-leaf parsley

sea salt and freshly ground black pepper

1   Trim off and discard the leafy fronds at the top of the fennel, then remove and discard the
    outer leaves. Slice each bulb in half lengthwise and then slice each half into quarters.

2   Heat 2 tablespoons of the oil in a heavy-bottom saucepan over low heat. Add the fennel,
    cover the pan with a lid, and cook, stirring occasionally, 5 to 6 minutes until the fennel is
    just starting to brown. Stir in the garlic and cook 30 seconds, then add the Savoy cabbage
    and chard and cook, covered, 3 minutes.

3   Pour in the stock, turn up the heat, and bring to a boil. Remove the lid, turn the heat down,
    and leave to simmer 10 to 12 minutes until most of the liquid evaporates and the vegetables
    are tender.

4   Meanwhile, heat the remaining oil in a heavy-bottom skillet. Add the pancetta and fry
    4 to 5 minutes until just crispy; remove from the pan and drain on paper towels.

5   Add the spinach to the pan of vegetables and, gently pressing the leaves down with the
    back of a wooden spoon, cook 2 to 3 minutes until it wilts. Remove from the heat, stir in the
    chopped parsley, and season lightly with salt and pepper. Stir in the crispy pancetta and
    serve, using a slotted spoon to drain the vegetables of any remaining liquid.

desserts

Creamy, crumbly, fruity, chocolatey, light and summery, or rich and

heavenly—whatever kind of dessert you're looking for, you'll find it here.

Choose from an array of cakes and tarts, including Rich Chocolate Tart,

baked desserts, such as Raspberry Soufflés, or quick treats, such as Mango

and Pistachio Fool. There are family favorites, too, such as Coconut Rice

Pudding, super-healthy options, like Fruit Kabobs with Raspberry Coulis,

and utterly indulgent dishes, such as Almond Cake with Passionfruit Syrup

or the meltingly delicious Chocolate Fondue with Fruit. Desserts burst with

intoxicating scents, colors, textures, and tastes and are usually far easier

to make than they appear. Most of these can be cooking away while you eat

your main course, or made in advance—so go for it!

flourless chocolate cake

PREPARATION TIME **10 MINUTES**   COOKING TIME **30 MINUTES**   SERVES **10**

7 tablespoons dairy-free margarine,
plus extra for greasing
8 ounces dairy-free dark chocolate,
with at least 70 percent cocoa solids
6 eggs, separated
²/₃ cup fruit sugar

Topping:
5 ounces dairy-free dark chocolate,
with at least 70 percent cocoa solids
scant ¹/₂ cup chestnut puree
3 tablespoons fruit sugar
2 tablespoons dairy-free margarine

1   Preheat the oven to 350°F. Lightly grease an 8-inch springform cake pan with dairy-free margarine and line the bottom with a circle of baking parchment.

2   Break the chocolate into small pieces and place in a large heatproof bowl. Rest the bowl over a pan of gently simmering water, making sure the bottom of the bowl does not touch the water; stir from time to time until the chocolate melts. Add the margarine to the bowl and continue stirring occasionally until it completely melts and is mixed in with the chocolate; remove from the heat.

3   Put the egg whites in a mixing bowl and whisk using an electric mixer until they form stiff peaks. Add the sugar and continue whisking until they form glossy peaks.

4   Lightly beat the egg yolks in another bowl, then stir into the melted chocolate mixture until well blended. With a large metal spoon, carefully fold in the whisked egg whites until they are thoroughly mixed in.

5   Pour the batter into the prepared cake pan and bake in the hot oven 25 to 30 minutes until risen and cooked around the side, but still slightly soft in the middle. Insert a skewer into the middle of the cake and if there is only a little of the cake batter sticking to it, the cake is ready. Take the cake out of the oven and leave to cool in the pan about 5 minutes, then turn out onto a wire rack and leave to cool completely.

6   Meanwhile, prepare the topping. Melt the chocolate as above. Add the chestnut puree and sugar and stir well, then stir in the margarine until thoroughly blended. Remove from the heat, leave to cool, and serve with slices of cake.

cakes & tarts

desserts

almond cake with passionfruit syrup

PREPARATION TIME **10 MINUTES**   COOKING TIME **20 TO 25 MINUTES**   SERVES **6**

dairy-free margarine for greasing

4 eggs plus 6 egg yolks

$^1/_2$ teaspoon ground cinnamon

$^1/_2$ cup fruit sugar

heaped 2$^1/_2$ cups finely ground blanched almonds

7 tablespoons apple or mango juice

Passionfruit syrup:

10 passionfruits

$^1/_2$ cup apple or mango juice

6 tablespoons fruit sugar

1   Preheat the oven to 350°F. Lightly grease an 8-inch springform cake pan with dairy-free margarine and line the bottom with a circle of baking parchment.

2   Put the eggs and egg yolks in a large mixing bowl with the cinnamon and sugar. Using an electric mixer, whisk until the mixture is very thick and creamy and doubles in volume; when the whisk is lifted from the mixture, it should leave a ribbonlike trail. Fold in the ground almonds carefully, using a large metal spoon, then stir in the apple or mango juice until evenly mixed.

3   Tip the batter into the prepared cake pan and bake in the hot oven 20 to 25 minutes until it is golden and well risen and a metal skewer inserted into the middle comes out clean. Take the cake out of the oven, turn out onto a wire rack, and leave to cool a little.

4   Meanwhile, prepare the passionfruit syrup. Cut the passionfruits in half and scoop the seeds and pulp out into a heavy-bottom saucepan, discarding the skins. Stir in the apple or mango juice and the fruit sugar. Bring to the boil, then turn the heat down and leave to simmer 20 minutes until the liquid reduces by half; leave to cool a little.

5   While the cake is still warm, spread the warm passionfruit syrup over the top and serve.

cherry tart

PREPARATION TIME **15 MINUTES**   COOKING TIME **40 TO 45 MINUTES**
ADDITIONAL TIME **MAKING THE PASTRY DOUGH**   SERVES **6 TO 8**

5 tablespoons dairy-free margarine, plus extra
   for greasing
1 recipe quantity Sweet Rich Piecrust Dough
   (see page 22)
rice flour for dusting
2 ounces silken tofu

4 tablespoons soymilk
¹/₄ cup fruit sugar
1 teaspoon vanilla extract
4 egg yolks
2¹/₃ cups pitted and halved cherries

1   Preheat the oven to 400°F. Grease a 10-inch tart pan, 1¹/₄ inches deep, with dairy-free
    margarine.

2   Roll out the dough on a board liberally dusted with rice flour into a circle about ¹/₈ inch
    thick and 1¹/₄ inches larger all around than the pan to allow enough dough for the sides.
    Be careful, as the dough will still be slightly sticky. Place the pan upside down on top of
    the dough and trim around to neaten it, then turn the board over to drop it into the pan.
    Ease the dough into place, pressing down carefully to remove any air pockets.

3   Line the tart shell with a piece of baking parchment and cover with baking beans. Bake
    in the hot oven 10 to 12 minutes until just golden. Take the tart case out of the oven and
    remove the parchment and beans. Turn the oven down to 350°F.

4   Meanwhile, prepare the filling. Using a stick blender or blender, blend the tofu and soymilk
    together until smooth. Whisk the margarine and sugar together in a mixing bowl until light
    and fluffy. Beat in the vanilla extract and egg yolks, then pour in the tofu and soymilk
    mixture and beat again until thoroughly blended.

5   Arrange the cherries over the bottom of the tart shell and pour the filling mixture carefully
    over the top. Bake in the hot oven 25 to 30 minutes until the top is golden brown. Take the
    tart out of the oven and leave to cool in the pan until the filling has set, then carefully ease
    it out onto a plate, and serve.

tarte tatin

PREPARATION TIME **10 MINUTES**   COOKING TIME **40 TO 55 MINUTES**
ADDITIONAL TIME **MAKING THE PASTRY DOUGH**   SERVES **6**

5 tablespoons dairy-free margarine

¹/₂ cup fruit sugar

7 apples, peeled, cored, and cut in half

1 recipe quantity Tarte Tatin Pastry Dough

(see page 22)

rice flour for dusting

1   Melt the margarine gently in an 8-inch heavy-bottom skillet with an ovenproof handle. Sprinkle the sugar over the top, then arrange the apple halves, cut-side down, in one layer.

2   Cook over gentle heat 20 to 30 minutes until the apples are soft and golden and the liquid caramelizes; remove from the heat.

3   Preheat the oven to 425°F. Roll out the dough on a surface liberally dusted with rice flour into a circle that is slightly larger than the skillet. Be careful, as the dough will still be slightly sticky. Trim the dough neatly into a circle with a knife. Carefully lift the dough with a metal spatula and place it on top of the pan, completely covering the apples; tuck in the edge.

4   Place the pan in the hot oven and bake 20 to 25 minutes until the pastry is golden brown; take the tart out of the oven and leave to cool in the pan 2 minutes. Place a serving plate, upside-down, over the top of the pan, then, holding the pan and plate together, turn them over so the tarte tatin turns out onto the serving plate with the caramelized apples on top and serve.

rich chocolate tart

PREPARATION TIME **10 MINUTES**   COOKING TIME **30 TO 35 MINUTES**
ADDITIONAL TIME **MAKING THE PASTRY DOUGH**   SERVES **6 TO 8**

desserts

4 tablespoons dairy-free margarine, plus extra
    for greasing
1 recipe quantity Sweet Rich Piecrust Dough
    (see page 22)
rice flour for dusting
7 ounces dairy-free dark chocolate,
    with at least 70 percent cocoa solids

2 ounces silken tofu
5 tablespoons plus 1 teaspoon soymilk
4 egg yolks
3 tablespoons fruit sugar

1   Preheat the oven to 400°F. Grease a 10-inch tart pan, 1$^{1}/_{4}$ inches deep, with dairy-free margarine.

2   Roll out the dough on a board liberally dusted with rice flour into a circle about $^{1}/_{8}$ inch thick and 1$^{1}/_{4}$ inches larger all around than the pan to allow enough dough for the sides. Be careful, as the dough will still be slightly sticky. Place the pan face down on top of the dough and trim around to neaten it, then turn the board over to drop it into the pan. Ease the dough into place, pressing down carefully to remove any air pockets.

3   Line the tart shell with a piece of baking parchment and cover with baking beans. Bake in the hot oven 10 to 12 minutes until just golden. Take the tart shell out of the oven, remove the parchment and beans, and turn the oven down to 350°F.

4   Meanwhile, prepare the chocolate filling. Break the chocolate into pieces and put in a heat-proof bowl, then rest the bowl over a saucepan of gently simmering water, making sure the bottom of the bowl does not touch the water. Stir from time to time until the chocolate melts. Remove the chocolate from the heat and stir in the margarine until it melts. Using a stick blender or blender, blend the tofu and soymilk until smooth.

5   Whisk the egg yolks in a large bowl, then add the sugar and whisk again until thick and creamy. Beat in the milk and tofu mixture until smooth, then stir in the melted chocolate and margarine and mix until well blended.

6   Pour the filling into the tart shell. Bake in the hot oven 20 to 22 minutes until the filling is springy to the touch. Take the tart out of the oven and leave to cool in the pan until the filling has set, then ease out onto a plate and serve.

coconut rice pudding

PREPARATION TIME **5 MINUTES**   COOKING TIME **2 HOURS**   SERVES **4**

dairy-free margarine for greasing

3¹/₃ cups coconut milk

³/₄ cup soymilk

¹/₂ cup pudding rice

3¹/₂ tablespoons fruit sugar

3 star anise

1   Preheat the oven to 300°F. Lightly grease a 10-cup baking dish with dairy-free margarine. Mix the milks together in a bowl.

2   Put the rice in the prepared dish and mix in the sugar. Add the star anise, then pour the milk mixture over the top and stir. Bake in the warm oven 2 hours, stirring every 30 minutes.

3   Take the pudding out of the oven. Using a large metal spoon, remove and discard the layer of coconut oil that forms on the top, then remove and discard the star anise before serving.

raspberry soufflés

PREPARATION TIME **10 MINUTES**   COOKING TIME **12 TO 17 MINUTES**   SERVES **6**

dairy-free margarine for greasing

5 egg whites

¹/₂ cup fruit sugar

10 ounces raspberries

2 drops rosewater

1 teaspoon cornstarch

1 Preheat the oven to 350°F. Grease six large, deep 1¹/₂-cup ramekins or a 9-cup soufflé dish with dairy-free margarine.

2 In a clean bowl, whisk the egg whites using an electric mixer until they form stiff peaks. Add half the sugar and continue whisking until they form glossy peaks.

3 Place the raspberries and the remaining sugar in a small, heavy-bottom saucepan and heat gently over low heat 4 to 5 minutes until the fruit is soft. Stir in the rosewater, then strain the mixture through a nonmetallic strainer into a large mixing bowl. Mix 1 teaspoon water and the cornstarch together in a small bowl to make a smooth paste and whisk into the strained raspberry mixture.

4 Add one third of the whisked egg whites to the raspberry mixture and whisk until blended. With a metal spoon, carefully fold in the remaining egg whites until they are all thoroughly mixed in.

5 Pour the mixture into the prepared ramekins or soufflé dish and bake in the hot oven 8 to 12 minutes, depending on the size, until very lightly brown on top and well risen; take the soufflés out of the oven and serve immediately.

apricot clafoutis

PREPARATION TIME **10 MINUTES**   COOKING TIME **65 TO 70 MINUTES**   SERVES **4**

dairy-free margarine for greasing

1³/₄ pounds ripe apricots, cut in half vertically
    and pitted

3 tablespoons honey

4 eggs

¹/₂ cup fruit sugar

2¹/₂ tablespoons rice flour

4 tablespoons gram flour

2 cups soymilk

1   Preheat the oven to 350°F. Lightly grease an 11-cup baking dish with dairy-free margarine.

2   Arrange the apricots, cut-side up, in a baking tray. Drizzle the honey into the hollow in the middles of the apricot halves and bake in the hot oven 30 minutes.

3   Meanwhile, beat the eggs and sugar together in a mixing bowl with an electric mixer until thick and creamy. Sift in the flours and, with a metal spoon, carefully fold into the egg mixture. Stir in the soymilk, then place the batter in the refrigerator until the apricots are cooked.

4   Remove the baked apricots from the oven and turn the temperature up to 375°F. Transfer the apricots to the prepared dish and pour any honey remaining in the baking tray over. Pour the batter over the top and bake in the hot oven 35 to 40 minutes until well risen and set, with a golden-brown crust formed on the top. Take the clafoutis out of the oven and serve.

baked figs with yogurt and pine nuts

PREPARATION TIME **5 MINUTES**   COOKING TIME **30 TO 35 MINUTES**   SERVES **4**

12 ripe figs

3 tablespoons honey

$^1/_2$ cup pine nuts

1 cup soy yogurt

1   Preheat the oven to 350°F. Place the figs in a large baking dish and drizzle the honey over. Bake in the hot oven 30 to 35 minutes until the figs are tender and the juices evaporate.

2   Meanwhile, heat a heavy-bottom skillet over medium heat. Toss in the pine nuts and dry-fry, stirring constantly, until just beginning to brown; tip into a bowl.

3   When the figs are cooked, take them out of the oven and serve covered with yogurt and sprinkled with toasted pine nuts.

stuffed peaches

PREPARATION TIME **10 MINUTES**   COOKING TIME **30 TO 35 MINUTES**   SERVES **4**

baked desserts

dairy-free margarine for greasing

scant ¹/₂ cup finely ground blanched almonds

1 tablespoon date syrup

¹/₂ teaspoon vanilla extract

4 large ripe peaches, cut in half vertically

    and pitted

³/₄ cup organic dessert wine

1   Preheat the oven to 350°F. Lightly grease a large roasting pan with dairy-free margarine.

2   Place the ground almonds, date syrup, and vanilla extract in a mixing bowl and, using your fingers, rub the mixture together until well mixed. With a teaspoon, scoop a small circle of the flesh from the middle of each peach half, enlarging the hole left by the pit. Chop this flesh finely and stir into the almond mixture. Add scant ¹/₂ cup of the dessert wine and mix well.

3   Spoon 2 teaspoons of the almond mixture into the hole in the middle of each peach half. Place the peaches, cut-side up, in the prepared pan and bake in the hot oven 30 to 35 minutes until golden brown.

4   Take the peaches out of the oven. Place 2 stuffed peach halves on each plate, pour 1 tablespoon of the remaining dessert wine over them, and serve.

baked strawberries with gooseberry custard

PREPARATION TIME **10 MINUTES**   COOKING TIME **20 TO 25 MINUTES**   SERVES **4**

1³/₄ pounds strawberries, hulled

2 cups soymilk

1 tablespoon cornstarch

5 extra-large egg yolks

²/₃ cup fruit sugar

¹/₂ teaspoon vanilla extract

12 ounces gooseberries, topped and tailed

1   Preheat the oven to 325°F. Place the strawberries on a large sheet of baking parchment on a baking tray, bring the sides together to make a package, and tuck the ends under. Place in the hot oven and bake 20 to 25 minutes until the fruit is starting to soften, but still holds its shape.

2   Meanwhile, heat the soymilk in a heavy-bottom saucepan over low heat until almost boiling. While the milk is warming, mix the cornstarch and 1 tablespoon water together in a small bowl to form a smooth paste. Whisk the egg yolks, 4 tablespoons of the fruit sugar, and the cornstarch paste together in a large mixing bowl until the mixture thickens. Pour in the hot millk and stir until thoroughly mixed.

3   Pour the mixture into a clean saucepan, add the vanilla extract, and cook over low heat 10 to 15 minutes, stirring frequently, to form a thick custard. Be careful not overheat or it may curdle; if it does, use a whisk or electric mixer to make it smooth again.

4   While the custard is cooking, put the gooseberries in a heavy-bottom saucepan with 1 tablespoon water, bring to a boil, then turn the heat down and simmer 5 to 10 minutes until soft, pushing the fruit down with a wooden spoon as it cooks. Using a stick blender, blend the fruit to form a smooth puree. Alternatively, blend the fruit in a blender or food processor. Push through a strainer to remove the seeds, discard the pulp, and put in a clean bowl.

5   When the custard is cooked, stir it into the fruit puree along with the remaining sugar. Take the strawberries out of the oven and serve with the gooseberry custard.

fruit kabobs with raspberry coulis

PREPARATION TIME **10 MINUTES**   COOKING TIME **12 TO 15 MINUTES**   SERVES **4**

8 apricots, cut in half and pitted

3 peaches or nectarines, peeled, cut in half,
    and pitted, then each half cut into 4 pieces

1 pineapple

24 large strawberries, hulled

Raspberry coulis:

13 ounces raspberries

3 tablespoons fruit sugar

1   To make the coulis, place the raspberries and sugar in a heavy-bottom saucepan and cook gently over low heat 4 to 5 minutes. Push the mixture through a fine non-metallic strainer, discard the pulp and keep warm.

2   Place the apricots and peaches or nectarines in a large bowl. Trim the woody bottom and green top off the pineapple and, holding it upright, slice off and discard the skin, including the "eyes." Slice the flesh thickly lengthwise, then remove and discard the core. Chop the flesh into bite-size chunks. Add to the bowl of fruit with the strawberries.

3   Preheat the broiler to high. Thread the fruit pieces onto 8 long metal skewers, mixing the fruit pieces. Place on a broiler rack under the hot broiler and broil 4 to 5 minutes on each side.

4   Serve the fruit skewers with the raspberry coulis.

mango and pistachio fool

PREPARATION TIME **5 MINUTES, PLUS 2 HOURS CHILLING TIME**   SERVES **6**

4 tablespoons cornstarch

1 cup coconut cream

4 large ripe mangoes

¹/₃ cup shelled, unsalted pistachio nuts, finely chopped

2 to 3 tablespoons honey

1 Add 3 tablespoons water to the cornstarch in a small bowl and stir to form a smooth paste. Put the coconut cream in a heavy-bottom saucepan and heat gently, adding the cornstarch paste a little at a time and beating with a whisk throughout. Heat 5 to 6 minutes until the mixture is thick, then whisk thoroughly and leave to cool.

2 With a sharp knife, carefully slice the mangoes down the sides, avoiding the pit. Cut the flesh inside the slices into small squares, cutting down to the peel but not piercing it, and scoop it out with a spoon. Peel the remaining parts of the mangoes and cut the flesh off the stones.

3 Put all the mango flesh and the coconut mixture in a bowl with half the pistachios and blend together thoroughly with a stick blender. Alternatively, blend them in a blender or food processor. Add the honey to taste and blend quickly, then add the remaining pistachios, reserving 1 tablespoon for later, and stir thoroughly.

4 Spoon the fool into glasses or bowls and leave to chill in the refrigerator at least 2 hours. Sprinkle with the reserved pistachio nuts and serve.

chocolate fondue with fruit

PREPARATION TIME **10 MINUTES**   COOKING TIME **10 MINUTES**   SERVES **4**

1 pineapple

2 bananas, sliced into thick chunks

10 ounces soft fruit, such as strawberries, hulled,
    and grapes

10 ounces dairy-free dark chocolate,
    with at least 70 percent cocoa solids

1$^1/_2$ tablespoons blackstrap molasses or honey

2 cinnamon sticks

1   Trim the woody bottom and green top off the pineapple and, holding it upright, slice off and
    discard the skin, including the "eyes." Slice the flesh thickly lengthwise, then remove and
    discard the core. Chop the flesh into bite-size chunks and place in a large bowl, along with
    the bananas and soft fruit; toss gently to mix the fruit then transfer to a serving dish.

2   Break the chocolate into small pieces and place in a heatproof bowl. Rest the bowl over
    a pan of barely simmering water, making sure the bottom of the bowl does not touch the
    water, stirring from time to time until the chocolate melts.

3   Stir the molasses or honey into the chocolate, then push the cinnamon sticks into the
    mixture, making sure they are covered; leave to heat gently 4 to 5 minutes. Take the bowl
    off the heat and gradually stir in $^1/_2$ cup water to form a thick chocolate cream. Remove and
    discard the cinnamon sticks. Serve the fondue with fruit for dipping.

chocolate and coconut mousse

PREPARATION TIME **10 MINUTES**   COOKING TIME **10 MINUTES, PLUS 1 HOUR CHILLING TIME**   SERVES **6**

2 tablespoons cornstarch

1 cup coconut cream

7 ounces dairy-free, dark chocolate,
with at least 70 percent cocoa solids

3 eggs, separated

unsweetened coconut flakes, to serve

1   Add 1½ tablespoons water to the cornstarch in a small bowl and stir to form a smooth paste. Put the coconut cream in a heavy-bottom saucepan and heat gently, adding the cornstarch paste a little at a time and beating with a whisk throughout. Heat 5 to 6 minutes until the mixture is thick, then whisk thoroughly and leave to cool.

2   Break the chocolate into small pieces and place in a large, heatproof bowl. Rest the bowl over a pan of gently simmering water, making sure the bottom of the bowl does not touch the water, stirring from time to time until the chocolate melts.

3   Add the egg yolks to the chocolate, whisk thoroughly using an electric mixer, then remove from the heat, add the coconut mixture, and whisk thoroughly again.

4   Meanwhile, heat a heavy-bottom skillet over medium heat until hot. Add the coconut flakes and dry-fry until light brown, turning frequently to prevent burning. Tip the toasted flakes into a bowl.

5   Put the egg whites in a mixing bowl, clean the mixer, then whisk until they form stiff peaks. Using a large metal spoon, fold the egg whites into the chocolate mixture, one-third at a time, until they are all thoroughly mixed in.

6   Spoon into six ¾-cup ramekins and leave to chill in the refrigerator at least 1 hour. Sprinkle with the toasted coconut flakes and serve.

quick desserts

index

index

176

There are so many people to thank for helping me while I've been writing this book. Huge thanks go to Max and Annabel for their support, to all my wonderful family and friends who have turned up to taste the recipes, to Katharine for her biscuit testing and to my sister Kate for her advice. Enormous thanks go, also, to Bob, Duncan, Alex, and Roger for their unfailing support for this project, and to the team at DBP who have created such a beautiful book – especially Allee, Dan, William, Jenny, Ryan, Maddie, Christine, Beverly, Sarah, Kirty, Susie, Ingrid and Uzma. And deepest thanks to my husband, Peter, without whom this book would never have been written. His patience, support, and unfailing encouragement (even when I worked on the shoot list on our honeymoon) have been just wonderful.